I have twice had the privilege of hearing Alter Wiener tell the story of his experiences during the Holocaust. It is a tragic story, even terrifying, yet it is vitally important that coming generations, which will not have the opportunity to hear survivors in person, learn of it. Thankfully, they will now have that opportunity, through From a Name to a Number: A Holocaust Survivor's Autobiography. The author tells his story succinctly, in the same tone and style that he might use if speaking to an audience. The end result is a short book but not a quick read, for readers will wish to ponder the story presented here. Mr. Wiener prefaces his narrative with a plea for tolerance, directing it to a world that continues to be markedly intolerant. From a Name to a Number addresses the two primary imperatives of Holocaust literature – "Never Forget!" and "Never Again!"

Paul Kopperman
Professor of History
Oregon State University

There are many amazing stories of survival during the Holocaust and Alter Wiener's life, courage, and faith are among the most inspiring. Emerging from the human created hell, Alter has triumphed over those who forgot their human and divine image. In these pages he has written a true account of much that he suffered and endured, with the humor, thoughtfulness, and positive message that in this world of war and hatred is more urgent than ever.

Alon K. Raab
Lecturer, Dept. of Religious Studies,
University of California, Davis, CA

Alter Wiener tells a compelling, devastating story of his sufferings and the destruction of 123 of his family members by the Nazis in the Holocaust. His story is a persuasive rebuttal of all forms of ignorance that afflict humans today. Countless students have heard his story and many have told him of the crucial difference he made in their lives. No one can learn of Alter Wiener's story and be unmoved.

Michael R. Steele, Ph.D.
Distinguished University Professor
Pacific University, Forest Grove, OR

64735

FROM A NAME TO A NUMBER

A Holocaust Survivor's Autobiography

ALTER WIENER

authorHOUSE®

AuthorHouse™
1663 Liberty Drive
Bloomington, IN 47403
www.authorhouse.com
Phone: 1 (800) 839-8640

Book cover design by Julian Dobbie, Salem, Oregon

Published by AuthorHouse   02/28/2018

ISBN: 978-1-4259-9740-3 (sc)
ISBN: 978-1-4259-9745-8 (hc)
ISBN: 978-1-4520-9118-1 (e)

Library of Congress Control Number: 2007903821

Print information available on the last page.

This book is printed on acid-free paper.

IN MEMORY OF:

My mother, Pearl (Pepka) Wiener, nee Tilles—
Interred in Chrzanów, Poland.

Step-mother, Rachel Wiener, nee Wurtzel—
Murdered in the Holocaust.

Father, Mordechai-Markus (sobriquet Motel) Wiener—
Murdered by the Germans on September 11, 1939.

My brother, Shmuel—Murdered in the Holocaust.

My brother, Hirsh—Murdered in the Holocaust.

All my other relatives—Murdered in the Holocaust;
they had **no funeral**, there are **no graves** and
no anniversaries of their demise.

CONTENTS

PREFACE

I had lived in Forest Hills, New York for forty years and I had never been asked to share my life story with students or adults. Like many other Holocaust survivors, I focused on adjusting to a new life in a new country. I had a full-time job until the age of seventy-three, and then I left New York for Oregon.

I have never been able to bring down an iron curtain on my past. For me, the horrific memories from the Holocaust are still fresh. The ashes I rose from are still smoldering. I am tormented by memories even as I try to carry on with my life. I am crying in silence. I am still in pain, and I am draped in sadness. While grieving, I am also somewhat healed. Most members of my extended family have passed away, but their love remains, and our relationships will never end, because love is not mortal. The warmth that permeated our family is the anchor that I hang onto. The Holocaust is a ghastly and repulsive historical nightmare. Not all physical and mental scars can be completely healed with passing years; some extend through time. However, I cannot let grief immobilize me.

I realize that it is beyond the understanding of most people to fathom the horror and dread that I have witnessed and endured. The Holocaust is indeed beyond comprehension. My tribulations during the Holocaust are so removed from people's daily lives that those horrors sound unbelievable to them.

In April 2000, I moved to Hillsboro, Oregon where I met a Holocaust survivor who urged me to join the Oregon Holocaust Resource Center

(OHRC). I did, and soon became a member of the OHRC "Speakers Bureau." The speakers share their Holocaust experiences with young students and adults in the states of Oregon and Washington.

I have always been self-conscious of my limited vocabulary, my foreign accent, and my flawed diction. Had I been well-versed in the English language, I would have still felt uncomfortable to address audiences. However, I was coaxed by the coordinator of OHRC to give it a try, and I made my first presentation in December 2000 at Century High School in Hillsboro, Oregon.

Since then, I have shared my life story with about 300 audiences. Most of my listeners have been quite respectful and sympathetic, as reflected in their faces; sometimes with outrage and often with tears. They are captivated in their rapt attentiveness. The appreciation for my implicit and explicit messages is reflected in their verbal and written responses. I am very pleased when told by teachers that my presentation inspired even the most fidgety students.

I was not aware that my voice could have a positive impact on life audiences. I pray and hope that my harrowing story, which continues to be so difficult and painful to tell, will also propel the readers of *From a Name to a Number* to combat racism and prejudice whenever it appears, and with whomever it threatens. As students and adults respond appreciatively to my presentations, I sense an obligation to continue to share my life's story. As the Holocaust moves from a living memory into the archival past, and as the ranks of survivors are rapidly dwindling, it becomes imperative to perpetuate the Holocaust legacy. The Holocaust was indeed a Jewish tragedy, but also a tragedy for the entire civilized world to let it happen—an indelible human shame.

When I was liberated in May 1945, every ounce of me dreamed of a world without hatred, without prejudice, without persecution—an irenic environment. I still hold tightly to that dream. By defeating the Nazis, the Allies flicked the light switch for a free and enlightened world. I presumed then the Holocaust was an aberration of history, and I anticipated an encrusted postwar order of peace. Regretfully, it seems that the world is now moving towards darkness. It has not learned from the tragic lessons of World War II. The world is being put to a test today, and it falls into an abyss rather than rising to the height of human dignity. Arrogance is being fueled by oil and hubris by possessors of destructive weaponry .

In today's paradoxical world, there are boundless opportunities for a better future. However, political and racial conflicts, religious fundamentalists, and fanatical ideologists may lead to a global crematorium. It will be much more destructive than the one in Auschwitz. We are living in a time when a perilous situation may turn catastrophic and engulf all of us. The 27,000 nuclear warheads in various hands around the world have the potential to destroy entire continents. CBRN (chemical, biological, radiological and nuclear weapons) capabilities are being sought by terrorists. A single terrorist can carry out an act that may cause the death of millions. I have seen that man's capacity for evil has no limit, just as man's genius is not limited to reaching new heights in every human endeavor. The Holocaust legacy has an intrinsic value as a warning for the future.

Hitler's wars of conquest and the Holocaust left an indelible legacy which has been inherited, and will continue to be inherited, by every succeeding German generation. Today, many Germans would like to be exonerated for the most heinous crimes committed by their forebears. They would like to get beyond a brutal past—an unpalatable one. Holding future generations accountable for the atrocities of their ancestors is obviously not justified. However, the dark pages of Germany's past cannot be ripped from history books.

Many people turn away from the subject of the Holocaust, for they don't want to hear anymore about it. My children and most of my grandchildren show no desire to listen to and learn from my Holocaust experience. They do not enable me to share my pain with them. In my view, it is very important to expose the causes of the Nazi crimes and ensure that such causes are readily recognizable. In that fashion, if the seeds of genocide ever begin to appear, they can be identified and eradicated before they ripen. Only then can we feel secure that genocide will never happen again. Hitler's ideology and evil will have no future.

Our sages said thousands of years ago, "A smart man is the one who learns from his experience, but still the smartest is the one who learns from somebody else's experience." The Greeks have an adage, "We suffer on our way to wisdom." Albert Einstein said, "In the middle of difficulty, lies opportunity." It would be rewarding to me if my life story will elucidate the readers of this book—what intolerance may lead to and how reprehensible prejudice is.

The sole purpose of writing my autobiography is to share with the readers my bitter experiences which I hope that in so doing will help them to understand the scope of what had happened during the Holocaust. I strive to encourage my readers to think and to take actions so that another Holocaust does not happen again. In addition, it becomes imperative not to lose hope—to be appreciative of life, despite the adversities one has to face. My desire is to leave this world a better place than the one I inherited and experienced.

Every Holocaust survivor has a story to share. I have a deep sense of having a mission to share my life story. Many life stories will never be told, and many talents will never serve mankind, because so many talented individuals were murdered.

I am convinced that without a systematic approach to educate the young regarding the Holocaust, its meaning and lesson will fade. California and a few other states in the U.S. have passed laws stating that public schools must include the Holocaust legacy in their curriculum. I feel that it should become a mandatory subject to teach in all schools. This unfathomable reality is a part of history that is not to be forgotten.

I am pleased that the United Nation's declaration of setting January 27 (the anniversary of the liberation of Auschwitz death camp) as International Holocaust Remembrance Day. The November 1, 2005 resolution commends countries to establish programs of remembrance and education pertaining to the Holocaust. Secretary General Kofi Annan has pointed out the fact that the United Nations was founded on the ashes of the Holocaust. The adopted resolution states, "The U.N. bears a special responsibility to ensure that the Holocaust and its lessons are never forgotten and that this tragedy will forever serve as a warning to all people of the dangers of hatred, bigotry, racism and prejudice." Stressing the duty to remember and the duty to educate, the resolution rejects any denial of the Holocaust; condemns discrimination and violence based on religion or ethnicity. It calls for the U.N. establishment of outreach programs that encourage public engagement in Holocaust remembrance activities.

I saw a film depicting a cellist gone mad because the Nazis, upon learning his profession, crushed his fingers. In February 1943, a guard with an impish smile who had a little square mustache like Hitler, noticed that I had talked to another prisoner at work. For that infraction, (actually no reason or excuse needed) he summoned me to his post. While growling, he applied a lighted cigarette to my palm and punched me in the mouth, grumbling, *"Ferfluchte Jude, du wielst niemals wieder sprechen."* (Cursed Jew, you will never be able to talk again) He knocked out several of my teeth and caused other teeth to slant back. I was left to bleed and began wheezing. Nobody heard my cry of agony. All I could hear was my own heart pounding wildly. He probably would have killed me, but while hitting me, he somehow hurt his arm(s) and sought medical help. He knew how to inflict pain, but could not stand his own pain. I was dragged face downward by other inmates, to the camp. In spite of that Nazi's thrusting blow, his portended purpose had not materialized. I am not stifled—I do talk, and sometimes I do speak out. In the U.S., I enjoy the freedom to speak whenever and whomever I wish.

I am an ordinary person with an extraordinary past; my lecture presentations are based on an empirical foundation. I realize that sharing my story, although it does not alleviate my pain, propels a number of people to be more compassionate. Recounting my personal experiences often plays a positive role, like a teacher makes in a child's education. Many of my listeners become introspective and appreciative of the freedom they enjoy in this blessed U.S.A. where many ethnic, religious, and cultural groups live in a relatively harmonious environment.

Simon Dubnow, the renowned Jewish historian from Latvia, was killed by the Nazis in December 1941. His last words in Yiddish were *"shreibt unt farshreibt"* (Write and record!). He felt that those who witnessed the horrific events of the Holocaust have a sacred duty to tell what they experienced. I am one of the survivors who can still speak. If I do not write about my experiences now, my life story will never be told.

In the death chambers, once the doors were locked, the victims had only a few minutes to live, but some had the physical and moral strength to scratch the following phrases into the walls, *"Gedenkt unz," "Zychru otanu," "pamietaj nas," "Ne felejes el bennunket"*—remember us, remember the Nazi's cruelty.... It is gratifying to know that in the future, the past will be visual. My life story, as well as other Holocaust survivors' stories, have been taped, to which historians and others will have access.

There are only a few documents and pictures illustrated in this book because I only have a few. On arrival in Waldenburg concentration camp in September 1944, we were stripped of everything personal including meaningful photos to us, yet meaningless to the Germans. I do not have a birth certificate like any person in the modern world. At the age of eighty, I am not able to recount many family events, and many episodes have escaped my memory. Older relatives of mine who were more familiar with the woven strands of our family's history could have contributed to this book, but they are all dead.

To be monetarily rewarded for sharing my tragic experience just does not feel right. Therefore, I do not ask to be paid for my speaking engagements. The same principle applies to this book. I do not seek publicity, fame, or money. The income from this book, if any, will be donated to worthy causes. I am gratified that my spoken words have had a positive impact on people's minds and actions. I anticipate the same from my written words—some words are nothing but tears about my perennial pain.

This is not a story from history records etched on stone with a chisel, or written with a quill on parchment or papyrus, with a pencil or pen on paper. The accuracy of history records is often questioned. Print has been in existence for only 600 years. I am only in a position to aver that everything written in this non-fiction memoir is accurate (beside possible misspellings of German terms and imprecise dates) to the best of my ability and memory which is not infallible. Many memories vanished into oblivion and other memories are hard to bring out from dark cages. This is a chronological biography. It is my journey from childhood with a glimpse into the "old country." It is about my tribulations during the Holocaust and its ensuing odyssey.

ROOTS AND FAMILY IN CHRZANÓW, POLAND

I was born in 1926. My given name was Abraham Alter, and I was affectionately nicknamed Altuś. After the war, I just kept the name Alter, and left out the name Abraham. In Israel, it was suggested to change my first and last name to a Hebrew-sounding name. In the U.S., I was told that it would be easier for me if I Americanized my first and last names. However, I felt that by doing so, I would fail to carry on my family's surname, and that would be disrespectful to the murdered members of my family. I am the only Holocaust survivor of my immediate family, and the only link in a chain, which I am not supposed to break. I would rather die with the name given to me at birth.

MOTHER PEARL (PEPKA) WIENER, NEE TILLES

I do not know her date of birth. I do know that she died in January 1931, at the age of thirty-two. My mother's passing is the earliest event that I remember. Our maid yanked me home from *cheder* (a preschool class). She told my teacher that Mrs. Wiener had suddenly died. I am unable to picture her face, remember her smile, or imagine her arms around me. I cannot visualize her standing next to my cradle and singing lullabies to me. I became an orphan at the age of four.

Relatives, neighbors, and other people felt sorry for my unfortunate fate. When I was seven years old, a neighbor told me, "Many prominent people eulogized your mother. The entire neighborhood mourned her passing. She was an exceptionally bright woman, and a quiet, dignified giant. It is a pity that you will not be able to remember your mother's beauty and the love she showered upon you."

I have honored the memory of my mother, as traditionally required, by reciting a special mourner's prayer, the *Kadish* (consecration, the prayer for the dead) on every anniversary of her death, and on certain holidays. As a young boy, I visited her grave several times a year. This was a large Jewish cemetery. It was quite a difficult search for me to find Mom's resting place. I had to trudge in the deep snow. The cemetery was not manicured with paths and signs of direction, as it is today in most cemeteries. While trailing amid the sea of tombstones, I had creepy thoughts that someday one of the tombstones would bear my name.

My maternal grandparents and my mother's siblings showered me with love, intertwined with solace for my loss and theirs. In my uncle's (Laibel Tilles) home, there was a large wall portrait—still etched in my memory—of my beautiful mother. From my early years, I remember people telling me that my mother was a legendary beauty, and the prettiest woman in town. I could not picture her alive. I do recall, however, members of our family and others commenting about how my facial features resembled my mother. When I was nine years old, one neighbor told me that when my mother's corpse was lowered into the grave—they did not use caskets in those days. By Jewish tradition, the corpses were buried in shrouds—the gravediggers doubted that my mother's radiant face was indeed that of a dead person.

A relative mentioned to me that Dr. Adolph Reiser was not competent and had been negligent in treating my mother's heart problem. Malpractice claims were unheard of then. After Dr. Reiser's demise, I went to his grave to condemn him for failing to save my mother's life, and foolishly cursed his departed soul.

In 1945, after the war, I visited my mother's grave—most likely for the last time. I have been told by a friend who visited our hometown fifty-seven years later, that most tombstones in our abandoned cemetery had fallen or were vandalized. Intruders removed marble headstones and used them as building material.

My mother was not granted an ample life span for me to remember and emulate her. Nevertheless, I appreciate and cherish those values that she must have planted during my infancy, and in my formative years. The late Barry White, the singer, is best noted by his song, "Can't Get Enough Love, Babe." I have been lamenting for years the fact that I could not get enough love from my mother, due to her untimely death.

My mother had eleven siblings (to the best of my knowledge)— Shmuel (died in Palestine), Menachem, Chaya, and Rivkah died in Israel. Shaul, Shulem, Yechiel, Laibel, Beilu, Hinda and Tauba were murdered in the Holocaust.

STEPMOTHER RACHEL WIENER, NEE WURTZEL

My stepmother came into my life when I was five years old and when my brother, Shmuel, was nine. She introduced herself to us by saying, "I am Rachel, and wish to take care of you with devotion as your late mother Pearl did, blessed be her memory." A neighbor told me once that I had then kicked Rachel impetuously while sobbing, "I want my mother back!" Rachel had never failed to keep her promise and showered my older brother and I with unconditional love. Later on, when she gave birth to a son, Hirsh, she cared for the three of us with equal devotion.

Rachel never begrudged the wealthy, and had an abounded compassion for the poor. She handed out food to the needy and the sick in peaceful times, and continued to do so even during the war, when our own food supply was scarce. Before we sat down to eat our meal, Rachel carried out a plate of cooked food to a lonely tenant in our building. When a classmate of mine was sick, she sent me to his house with her baked goodies. There were no "get well cards" in those days.

We, the children, had a relatively comfortable life, but we were not protected from contact with reality. I recall her frequent use of locutions, "There are two ways to deal with the cold—put on a fur coat to be warm, or light a fire so that others can be warm, too." The element of self-sacrifice was part of her constitution. She had faith that somehow the Almighty would replenish her resources.

Rachel deemed God her father in heaven, and trusted him as a secure child trusts a dependable parent. Rachel never flaunted her own virtues and never derided others. She was inordinately kind, and would rather listen than talk. Her motto was, "We were given two ears, but only one tongue—to teach us that we should listen twice as much as we speak.

The key to all good human relations is listening. When your loved ones are talking, listen to them as if it were the last time hearing them."

Her sense of morality was to embrace everybody with kindness. She derived pleasure from imparting happiness to others. She shunned gossip and chitchat. I remember her saying, "Gossip harms three people—the one who is gossiping, the one who is listening, and the one who is being gossiped. Freedom of expression does not give us a right to insult and denigrate anybody."

Rachel never raised her voice in anger. Although we were not wayward kids, when we did misbehave, Rachel would wag a minatory finger, but she never lifted her hand to slap us. I remember her telling her sister, "I don't think that shouting in anger can help me or help the kids I am shouting at." Rachel believed that children should be addressed firmly and convincingly, rather than in a way that frightened them. This was in contrast to my father. He was strict with us, but used the rod sparingly. He believed that disciplined children would eventually grow up to be good and happy adults.

Harsh words were not part of Rachel's vocabulary. Everybody whom I remember was cursing the German oppressors, but not Rachel. Reading about the German ubiquitous victories, she told us the story of the battle of Trafalgar on Napoleon's Island. The British Navy destroyed the French and Spanish fleets, but Horatio Nelson, the greatest of the English admirals fell mortally wounded. "This will happen to Hitler; he is a *Rasha Raa*, (doubly wicked). He is wicked to God and men," Rachel said.

I do not know if Rachel was a graduate of any school. Schooling was not mandatory when and where Rachel grew up, especially for girls. Still, I do recall observing her reading whenever she had free time to do so. She once told my uncle, David, "If I didn't have other duties, I would physically chain myself to a book." Rachel's passion for books was contagious. "There must be something good about it that mom was so obsessed with it," my brother observed.

The values Rachel instilled in me are as important to me as my limbs. She has not just been a candle, but a torch in my life. Rachel left a profound impact, extending well into my adulthood. Her lessons of forgiveness, humility, meekness, steadfastness, and moral principals became my beacon in times of darkness. Rachel believed in dignity through simplicity. Her stark moral clarity continues to represent all the meritorious moral standards that I have been trying to emulate and live by until the end of my days.

Rachel was an ardent Zionist and had a clear conviction that there was no assured future for the Jewry in Poland. She had a prophetic vision about an approaching calamity. As it turned out, Rachel presciently forecasted our predicament for the future. She was realistic to a fault. Many times, she expressed her desire to move to Palestine. It was her dream! A second option she suggested, was to move to the U.S. where her sister, Shaindel, lived, with whom she was very close. My father, on the other hand, felt attached to Chrzanów where his ancestors had lived for many generations. He owned inherited property, which was a landmark in our town. Had my father consented to Rachel's wishes and left Poland before the war, my immediate family would not have been annihilated in the Holocaust.

When the Nazis murdered my father, Rachel could have walked away from the onerous burden of taking care of me when I was thirteen, and my older brother at the age of seventeen, but she had chosen to remain attached to her stepchildren with all the burdensome consequences. Rachel made every effort to make no distinction in caring for her stepchildren as she did for her own child.

On February 18, 1943 (Hebrew calendar Kav-Gimel Addar), Rachel and her son, at the age of nine, were rounded up and deported to Auschwitz with the last *Ausssidlung,* (expulsion) of Jews from Chrzanów. At that time, the town became *judenfrei* (free of Jews). Rachel's entire paternal and maternal families perished in the Holocaust.

For me, taking a shower is an appreciative luxury. I remember how we washed ourselves when there was no plumbing in our house in Chrzanów, and also how uncomfortable and ominous the shower rooms were in the concentration camps. However, today, when I look at the showerhead, I often visualize how my stepmother and her nine-year-old son died when, not water but Zyclon B—a cyanide-based pesticide—secreted from the showerheads. How much did they suffer by fighting for breath, for several minutes, before the last clawing, convulsive moment of suffocation occurred?

Rachel would say, "Never abandon your dreams; dwell on positive thoughts; you lose nothing by keeping your hopes alive! The adversities

we face are passing phases that will be followed by fortunate events."
I wanted to inscribe those adages on her headstone, but she had no
grave, just as the six millions of Holocaust victims, have none. I have
never met another woman of such faith, intelligence, and strength as
she had. She was noble without pretense, and regal in her simplicity.
She was the epitome of humanity, love, and devotion.

MY FATHER—MORDECHAI-MARKUS (SOBRIQUET MOTIL) WIENER

My father never took me to a baseball game or any other sporting
event. We never visited a museum, exhibition, park, zoo, swimming
pool, movie house, or a concert hall. Very few such places, if any, existed
in Chrzanów, when I grew up. My father did not buy me games—
very few were available or affordable back then. Little boys and girls
improvised with gravel and sticks made up their own games. Collecting
and exchanging stamps was a popular hobby. I never watched a parade
with my father, but I never missed watching him to see what was
important to him like his intense piety. He prayed three times a day
and observed every tenet of his faith with unswerving devotion. He
derived joy from his faith. Likewise, his devotion to his family was
compelling. Once, I remember him saying, "A man who does not care
for his own family is worse than an unbeliever in God."

He always got up early, before anybody else in the family. He washed
and did not shave—he grew a beard—and went to the synagogue
to pray. When he returned from prayer, my stepmother served him
breakfast. My father would then leave for his store, which was located
in the front of the lower level of our building. He owned this building,
and it was where my paternal family had lived for generations.

Father worked long hours to provide us with a decent living. We
never heard a single complaint about his heavy workload. I remember
him quoting Psalms 128: verse 2, "When you eat the labor of your
hands, you shall be happy." He valued hard work, honesty, patience,
thrift, charity, and tenacity. His sacred values were faith, justice, and
love for fellow man. He often quoted from the Ethics of our Fathers
(1.14), "If I am not for myself who will be? But if I am for myself only,
what am I?" My father was a humbled intellectual. He would exhort us
to learn; inculcating that **the real possession of man is not what he**

12

owns but what he knows. He imbued my brother and I with a sense of religious and intellectual purpose. Every Saturday he asked me to give him a full account of my studies, in public school, in *Cheder*, and my homework. He touted my achievements, and when I brought home a good report card, I was rewarded with a chocolate bar. Occasionally, my father took me for a stroll on *Aleja Henryka*, the most beautiful avenue in the town, where he bought me an ice cream or an éclair. Whenever my behavior exceptionally pleased my father, he gave me change to buy some pastry from Reb Moyshe Hochbaum. Mr. Hochbaum, a well-known scholar, was also a confectioner.

I never saw my father idle. His mottoes were, "Idleness is the killer of the soul. If you have time, don't waste it because every moment is precious. No sense to brood and no good to be bored." My father kept clear from cantankerous people. He often quoted Proverbs 18: verse 21, *Mavet Vehachaim bidei Halashon* (Death and life are in the power of the tongue). In other words, there are consequences to what you say or do not say. He would never gossip.

Compassion and charity were essential to my father's conduct. We had a homeless person or an out-of-town student—there were no dormitories attached to the houses of learning—at our dinner table every Friday night and Saturday noon. Many of the poor and vagrants would beseech congregants in the synagogue to accommodate them for a Sabbath, or holiday meal. My father always invited one or two of those unfortunates to come with him. He was glad to share a meal with those who could not afford one. Father's dinner conversations were animated without being verbose. He made the guests feel welcome and taught us children to be respectful to strangers. *Hachnasat Orchim* (hospitality to guests) was a command. The table discussions—never arguments—were about politics, assimilation, anti-Semitism, and the meaning of faith, justice, etc. My father was open-minded and was interested in thoughts of all of us around the table. After the meal, my father escorted the guests to the door and gave each one a little bag with extra food. He once said, "If I had a remedy for cancer or any other disease and would not share, what kind of human being would I be? If I am financially comfortable, is it not incumbent upon me to help the indigents? It is expected from me, and I like to give *tzedakah* (charity) because when a man dies, he takes nothing with him. All he

13

takes is what he had given." *Tzedakah* in Hebrew means not just charity but also righteousness, justice and fairness.

Father's love and respect for his wife, my stepmother, was obvious and intense. He always praised Rachel's intellectual curiosity. My father was never romantic with her in front of us children. In the culture I grew up in, people did not publicly embrace, kiss, or show passionate affection. Both of our parents were bound to each other at the deepest level. I cannot recall hearing one argument or the utterance of a harsh word between them. No telephones were available in those days, so my parents kept contact by an installed tube in the wall between our apartment on the upper floor and father's store on the lower floor. My stepmother inquired often to be assured that her husband was not hungry or thirsty.

My dad adhered religiously to the fifth commandment of the Bible, "Honor your father and mother." I remember him visiting his ailing mother every day. Before he left for work, he made sure that his mother's needs had been met. Many children nowadays do not see it as an obligation, and do not commit themselves to caring for their elderly parents. Even in China and Japan, the ancient assurance of care in old age has foundered. My father told me once, "Your grandmother is now as a young child is. She depends on me as you do. I would never neglect her, just as I would never abandon you. It is my duty to take care of both of you with the same sacred devotion. It is written that it is a divine mandate for us to show thoughtfulness, dignity, and compassion to those who brought us into the world. Children should never disappoint parents; children must make their parents proud of their offspring."

We lived in a strongly patriarchal society that revered the elderly, for whom my father had the highest esteem. He often quoted Leviticus 19:32, "You shall rise up before the aged and show deference to the old." On the eve of the New Year, I had to knock at the door of every tenant—twenty-four tenants in our building—to wish them a Happy New Year. The young were reared to be deferential to their parents, grandparents, teachers, and the elderly. I am moored to those beautiful values. Father was a disciplinarian, like most fathers were then. He taught me discipline and accountability. By being disciplined at home and school, we also learned to respect law and order everywhere. Nevertheless, my father was gentle, unfailingly polite, decent, kind, and generous. He had respect for the living and for the departed. He would insist that my older brother and I visit our mother's grave and the graves of other relatives, several times a year.

My father preached the Christian dictum, "Love the sinner and hate the sin." He added his own version, "Hate hatred and shun violence!" My father was indeed my principal teacher by exemplary conduct. As a *horeh* (parent), he was also my teacher (in Hebrew, *horeh* means both parent and teacher). Although he seldom spent time with me, I knew that he loved me deeply and tenderly, by the way he gazed at me. The beam of light emanating from him still illuminates my labyrinthine life.

On September 11, 1939, my father, we affectionately called him *tatishi*, was murdered by German soldiers. (See: The Turning Point in my Life.) This put my life in tatters! I was cut off from the best source of love and values, which he instilled in me during the first thirteen years of my life. His decency will always be the compass that guides me through adversity and confusion. I wish I would have had more years to prove to my father that I had indeed been a dutiful, and loving son. I owe him an enormous debt. Some values are taught with words, and my father transmitted them to me mostly by example.

My father's five brothers—Nathan, Samuel, Chaim-Usher, David and Yechiel were all murdered in the Holocaust. His sole sister, Chaya Seifman, had died some years before the war.

GRANDPARENTS HIRSH-ZVI AND SHAINDL WIENER

My paternal grandfather passed away when I was a baby. My grandmother died when I was a little kid. I cried and my stepmother told me, "Grandma is now with God. We have to be grateful for the time she was here with us." Regretfully, I do not know much about their life. I just remember the plaques in the school citing my grandparents for their contributions.

GREAT-GRANDFATHER ABRAHAM ALTER WIENER

My great-grandfather was a very respected and influential man in Chrzanów. His accomplishments were engraved on the headstone at his mausoleum, which I visited whenever I was at the cemetery to visit my mother's grave. I recall being beaten up by a schoolmate when I irritated him by boasting that my great-grandfather was resting in a mausoleum, while his great-grandfather was buried in a simple grave.

Several houses of prayer and learning bore plaques dedicated to the memory of my great-grandfather which recognized his support. I was proud to be a great-grandson of such a renowned man. When I was introduced to older people, they would tell me, "Carrying your great-grandfather's name obliges you to live up to his stature. Hopefully you will grow up to be a man of probity and piety as he was."

My great-grandfather had twenty-eight children. His first wife, Rebecca, died after bearing fourteen children. His second wife, Yochevet, also had fourteen children. Nine children died in infancy. High mortality in infancy was common in the nineteenth century. The last surviving child, Chaikah Lednitzer (nee Wiener), lived in Forest Hills, New York when I arrived. I wonder how my great-grandparents managed having so many kids to take care of. There was no running water, no diapers, no washers, and no cars, etc., in those days.

MATERNAL GRANDPARENTS, LAIZER AND LEAH TILLES

My maternal grandparents became my temporary guardians after my mother's death. The Tilles family was poor. I do not recall ever having received a toy or a game from them. A piece of cake meant a lot to me. During the war, a small piece of bread was a great gift. Every weekend my older brother and I would walk a mile to pay them a visit. They came to our house only once when I had broken my leg. In those days, children and grandchildren customarily paid frequent visits to their parents and grandparents, out of deference. It was not the other way around, as it is nowadays. I shall never forget my beloved pious, poor, and dignified grandparents. They were murdered in the Holocaust. I still see them often in my dreams.

MOTHER'S SISTER—CHAYA

Chaya, one of my mother's sisters, was married to Max Alexandrowitz, a policeman in the city of Haifa. The police force in Palestine included British, Jews and Arabs. Max, who emigrated from Germany to Palestine in his early teens, was a very talented man, a

My maternal grandparents were murdered in Auschwitz. I received these photos in 2001 from my cousin, Asher, who lives in the U.S.A.

powerful intellect, and he spoke several languages. Max died in 1939 from a militant Arab's bullets on a Haifa street, where Jews and Arabs had been living in a relative peaceful city. Chaya was pregnant with her first child, Gila, when the tragic event occurred. Gila Almagor is a famous actress, on stage and screen. She lives in Israel.

These photos show the funeral for my uncle Max in Haifa, Palestine in 1939. My aunt, Chaya, gave me these pictures in 1947.

MY CHILDHOOD IN
CHRZANÓW, POLAND

Chrzanów is located in the southwest corner of Poland, between Kraków and Katowice. In the sixteenth century, it was part of Eastern Upper Silesia Galicia. Poland regained its independence on November 11, 1918. In my time, the population in Chrzanów was about 20,000—half Jewish and half Roman Catholic.

In Chrzanów, most people were poor. Some could be categorized as middle-class. Very few were wealthy. The majority of the population led a religious life immersed in rich folklore. My father's family was considered wealthy. My mother's family was very poor. Deep rivers of poverty were flowing in most towns across Poland.

I attended an elementary public school in the morning, six days a week. In the afternoons, I went to a *cheder* (a religious class). I was expected to behave in schools as I was expected to behave at home, otherwise I would be punished in both places. There was plenty of homework. In retrospect, I am struck by how much responsibility we had as young kids.

I learned Yiddish and how to pray in Hebrew. I studied the Pentateuch, the five books of Moses, with Rashi's commentary. I liked to read the Ethics of our Fathers and I still do. It is full of classical wisdom. I still remember by heart several chapters from the Psalms. The Yiddish language was the religious and cultural substrata of the Jewish community. Most Jews conversed and dealt among themselves in Yiddish, the language that evolved in Eastern Europe, through centuries in the Diaspora. All schools, public as well as parochial, were non-coed.

Chrzanów was a small town, but not a piddling one. The first factory in Poland for the production of locomotives, *Fablok,* was located in Chrzanów.

The Germans invaded Chrzanów on September 4, 1939. It thus became part of the *Deutsche Reich* (the German Third Reich). Chrzanów was Germanized to Krenau.

THE CHRZANÓW THAT I REMEMBER

There was a house of worship in the rear;
    it was to all of us very dear.
Faith and ethics ran deep; daily prayers
    I would never leap.
Our father in heaven was king of the
    universe we all did fear.
Our father at home was the head of the
    household we all did revere.
We didn't wait for Mother's Day or
    Father's Day to say that we care.
Commercialized flowers, fancy confections,
    and cards were just not there.
Very rarely did we get presents.
None of my friends had divorced parents.
We did not have a car. There were no buses and
    no subways—just horses and buggies.
We had no washer and no dryer; our laundry
    was scrubbed on washboards.
Shoes were custom-made by a shoemaker.
    There were no shoe stores.
Suits were custom-made by a tailor. There
    were no department stores.
There were no refrigerators, no videos, and no audios.
There were no planes and no boats; no
    telephones, and no cell phones

There was a bookcase from wall-to-
    wall to enrich our minds.
A happier home you could never find.
    Grace and love knew no bounds.
Our luxuries were few indeed; yet
    somehow we filled every need.
Water to drink, cook, and wash, we
    fetched from the town's well.
Un-pasteurized milk we got out of heavy
    round metal milk churns.
We never dined outside. Mother cooked everyday.
She kneaded dough for macaroni and
    baked cakes for Saturday.
She baked *Challah* (braided bread) for
    every Sabbath and holiday.
The smell of her cooking and baking are
    closely linked in my memory.
We lived as happily as can be, in what
    is now called poverty.
We were content, you may be sure. My
    parents were very charitable.
Every Saturday, at our table, a homeless
    person felt respectable.

I have been privileged to live in an era of dramatic achievement by the human genius. Remarkable progress has been made in technology, medicine, science and in many other areas of human endeavor. I have also witnessed unprecedented human cruelty. I lived in a time when Jews were pillaged and suppressed, and a third of its people annihilated. Now, as the end of my life approaches, the more appreciative I am for the values instilled in me at the beginning of my life. The aroma of my family's home and the communal spirit of my hometown Chrzanów have not dissipated. As time moves on, nothing stays the same, but I am still standing in my nostalgic lane. My childhood memories are woven into my soul.

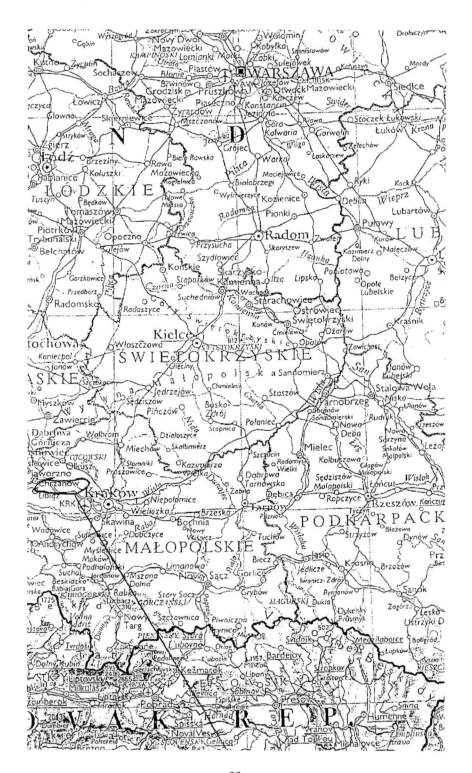

THE TURNING POINT IN MY LIFE

THE MURDER OF MY FATHER

The devastating impact of World War II—
the murder of my father on September 11, 1939.

On September 1, 1939, the German Army attacked and invaded Poland. On the same day, German fliers bombarded the Tzebinia railroad station, three miles from Chrzanów. No Polish fighter-planes or anti-aircraft artillery engaged them. The poorly equipped Polish defense was in no position to challenge the mighty German Air Force.

Since our town was close to the German border, many residents tried to flee into the interior and the countryside of Poland, to be as far away as possible from the invading enemy. Panic struck all residents of Chrzanów. We witnessed long caravans of horse-drawn wagons, jammed with people and their belongings. Evacuees from the border, streamed through our town. Chaos, confusion, and ominous rumors enveloped the population. Fear of the known and unknown were mirrored in the faces of all. Everybody was scared and on edge. Most governmental offices became dysfunctional. A crisis mode permeated the town. German warplanes appeared, and the sky was humming. There was nothing on the horizon to cheer up the gloomy population of Chrzanów. It was just a harrowing time.

Many people left their homes and most of their possessions. They tried to get away from the ominous invasion. Very few trucks or cars were available and most trains had stopped running. Carts, bicycles, wheelbarrows, and horse-drawn wagons were used to escape, or people just trudged away.

My father hired a Polish coachman with a horse-drawn carriage. My stepmother, Rachel, my older brother, Shmuel, my younger brother, Hirsh, and myself "lived" for several days and nights on that carriage. Our father did not join us because the Polish retreating army had ordered him to stay and provide them with provisions from his grocery business. All major roads were jammed with refugees. Many soldiers from the disintegrating Polish Army took off their uniforms and mingled with the masses of civilians. It did not bode well for Poland's ability to resist the German onslaught. When we reached the little town of Dombrowa, near Tarnów (where my stepmother's siblings still resided), we discovered that the Germans had already overrun that town. By fleeing, we did not escape the German menace.

We stayed in that illusory refuge for about three months. When we finally got back to our apartment, we found that it had been looted, and all the shelves in my father's store were emptied by the invaders and by some Poles. All the business records had vanished, which left us no way to collect what was owed to us. In those days, most wholesale businesses were conducted on credit, and recorded on paper ledgers. My stepmother, Rachel, said to us, "Don't worry children, possessions can be replaced. God will compensate us with a better livelihood. Trust the almighty!"

We expected our father to be at home but we could not find him. No matter where we inquired, nobody could tell us his whereabouts. His disappearance became our main concern. We prayed and hoped that our father would eventually show up. In November 1939, a member of the *Judenrat*, Jewish Community Council told my stepmother that at the outskirts of our town, in Trzebina, there was a pit of unidentified victims.

Thirty-eight people were picked up at random and were shot. My father was shot on September 11, 1939. He was left to bleed to death. One of those captives pretended to be dead, and managed to escape during the night. Thirty-seven victims were thrown into a pit. They were murdered for no other reason than to sow fear, panic, and subjugation among the populace, especially the Jewish inhabitants. That crime was committed by some cruel, heartless, and callous *Deutsche Wermacht* (soldiers of the German army). The soldiers were *schadenfreude* (taking pleasure in someone else's misery). They amused themselves while murdering innocent people.

The German commander of the local *Polizei* (police), along with an intermediary of the *Judenrat,* agreed to allow the pit to be opened and have the exhumed bodies given a proper burial. This was not an entirely magnanimous gesture on the part of the Germans. They were responding to Poles living in the neighborhood of the pit, who complained about a stench that stemmed from the fact that the rain had depleted the top soil of the pit.

"So, if you would like to know whether your husband is one of the victims, you will have to be present at the exhumation," my stepmother was told. In addition, the local rabbinical council ruled that it was imperative for the wives to identify their husbands' bodies as a prerequisite for possible remarriage in the future. That distressing requirement of identifying bodies made our entire family shiver with fear and horror.

The following morning, my stepmother, my older brother, and I went to the location of that pit. Without mechanized excavating equipment for such a task, several volunteers arduously exhumed the bodies with shovels and their hands. There was no medical examiner or coroner present, and no DNA existed in those days. It took a long time to identify the partially decomposed corpses. It was a very gruesome sight. I was thirteen years old and watched my stepmother collapse when she identified my father's body. She recognized certain familiar items that she had found in his clothing. I was horrified! I always remember the defining image of that cataclysmic event. It is deeply etched in my memory. I have been haunted by flashbacks and nightmares to this very day. That tragedy took place sixty-seven years ago, and it feels sometimes as if it had just happened. My emotions are as raw and painful as they were in 1939.

We silently trudged our way back home through torrential rain. There was no transportation available. Our tears intertwined with the rain during the soggy three- mile tedious walk. There was much to be said, but the three of us were speechless. I could not fall asleep that night. I was frightened, devastated, and overwhelmed.

The following day, thirty-seven caskets were brought to the Jewish cemetery in Chrzanów, for burial. Traditionally, the dead were buried without a casket, but the condition of partially decomposed bodies necessitated putting the victims in wooden caskets. The victims ranged in age from twenty to seventy. Several corpses had never been identified. In absence of heavy earth-moving equipment, it took many hours to prepare a mass grave. I was standing next to my father's casket and wondered whether my father was really lying inside that casket. I was enveloped in grief and numbness. I broke down and began weeping uncontrollably. My tears flowed non-stop and I did not care. There was no one who could put his arms around me. I was in dire need for somebody to reach out and tell me how to accept the bitter reality. I was whispering, praying, and staring, fixed on the coffin. "Daddy, why did they kill you? What have you done to deserve such a terrible punishment? Is it a crime to be a Jew?" In school, I learned that God rewards the good and punishes the wicked. My father was a pious and decent man, so why was he snatched away from me? That question has been vibrating in my mind ever since, as have all the other terrible events that ensued.

One-by-one, the coffins were lowered into the mass grave in the presence of hundreds of people from the community. The cantor, with a tremulous voice, chanted the *El Maleh Rachamim* (God, full of compassion), the prayer for the dead. All the freshly bereaved orphans and parents wept, while reciting the *Kaddish* (liturgical doxology), the mourners' prayer, in unison. With a heavy heart, I flung dirt, as is customary in Jewish tradition, onto my father's coffin, who laid entombed alongside the other thirty-six victims' coffins. As dirt was being shoveled onto the coffins, so was my orphaned future being filled with fear and anxiety! It was daunting to envision my life without the love and sustenance provided by a caring father. To me, everything seemed terribly muddy and frightening. I could not imagine a future without my father. I prayed in my heart, pleading with God to stay near me from then on. With a broken heart and spirit, my brother and I walked back home. Grief pulled life out of me. Both of us were engrossed in our unbearable sadness. I was scared to talk.

From the Left: My father; Mr. Gross, a family friend; and Shaul Tilles, my mother's brother. This photo was taken in Krenica, Poland (a resort) sometime in the late 1930s. My uncle, Menachem Tilles, who emigrated to Palestine in the 1930s before WWII, gave me this picture (from his album).

My father is listed #23 of the 37 victims; ten are unknown.

1946 - Unveiling of the monument for the 37 victims slaughtered in Trzebinia - September 1939.

That event shook my world to its foundations. I felt robbed of the sense of peace and love. My joy turned to sorrow. From that day in November 1939, the day of my father's burial, all my days were dark. There was not one flicker of sunshine until the day of liberation on May 9, 1945.

A German decree forced all the synagogues to permanently close their doors. Neighbors and friends came to our apartment, morning and evenings, to gather a *Minyan* (a quorum of ten adult males), required for communal prayer. This enabled my brother and I to recite the <u>*Kaddish*</u>, the prayer for mourners.

In the absence of the head of the household, we no longer had a breadwinner in the family. I was too young to be involved in managing the household. I did not know then, and I continue to wonder, how my stepmother managed to feed us.

The Passover night in April 1940, is a night I shall never forget. My father's chair at the dinner table was empty, and nobody else could take his seat to conduct the *Seder*. In normal times, in deference to the head of the household, nobody ever sat in his chair. This was a traditional custom. In Judaism, the *Seder*—commemorating the Exodus of the Jews from Egypt—is observed on Passover. The retelling of the story how the Jews were delivered from slavery is a festive occasion that brings families together. However, for my family, that first Passover night following my father's death was a night of lamentation, not celebration. My stepmother lamented, "The king of the house is absent and so is his shining crown. Daddy cannot be replaced! This is God's will and God will get us through this." Our wailing was louder than the prayers. That Passover was a melancholic atmosphere—a classic portrait of a grieving family. Rachel spent her days and nights trying to come to grips with her loss, and our loss.

The brutal murder of my father was a turning point in my life. It is an event that I shall mourn for the rest of my life.

PERSECUTION/DEPORTATION/
INCARCERATION

PERSECUTION IN CHRZANÓW

From the first day of the occupation, we were plagued with numerous decrees, issued by an officer of the occupying forces in our town. They were posted on walls and boards in public places. Most decrees were addressed to the Jewish community. This was the beginning of our ghettoization. Jews who had not noticed the new announcements and failed to follow them were consequently punished. With the absence of radio, many just missed reading the new edicts. However, that was no excuse. Jews were expected to "keep up" with the latest proclamations. The Jewish community was subjected to frequent curfews. When there was no curfew, most people were fearful to venture outside. They stayed indoors and out of sight, to avoid anyone in uniform. The newer announcements were always more ominous than the previous ones. Vicious posters were placed throughout the city. I remember one cartoon where the caption read, "The Jews are our curse." The normalcy of religious, cultural, and communal life ended. The occupation was depressing for all residents but the oppression of the Jews was the worst. The arbitrary became the legitimate policy of the occupying authorities.

I was banned from attending school. The Jewish community's fortress of piety had been destroyed by the sacrilegious Third Reich. Jews who possessed any valuables sold them, at bargain prices, to Poles for basic food. Jews were forbidden to travel, to assemble, to visit parks, playgrounds, cinemas, or theaters. Jews could not own a radio, a car, or a motorcycle. Those coercive measures restricted our freedom to move. Many Jewish businesses were confiscated or "Aryanized." The few who were rich before the war now joined the many poor in becoming destitute. Penury permeated the Jewish community. Most vital commodities were nonexistent. Being denied the means of sustaining life, many Jews became prone to starvation. As the winter approached, some froze to death. A few committed suicide. Not one benevolent organization from the outside world came to help our destitute community. Hopes for relief were dashed.

In May 1940, several priests and members of the Polish intelligentsia and Catholic clergy in our town were executed. By that time, thirty-eight priests had been executed and hundreds of clerics imprisoned, as it was reported to Pope Pius XII by the Polish Primate Cardinal Hlond.

The persecution aimed at the Jewish community brought vulnerability and dysfunction. Very few Jewish women gave birth. Many children were inflicted with rickets due to an inadequate intake of vitamin D. We all withered on meager food rations. Jews had to wear an armband with a blue Star of David. Later, it changed to a yellow Star of David. It was a crime if a Jew failed or rather, forgot to wear it. New rules forbade us to live, or even walk through certain sections of the town. We were ordered to take off our caps or hats and bow to any passing German. Nobody dared to raise a voice in protest. Everybody was bowed down, prostrated, and stifled. There was no other voice except the brutal German's voice. The abominable decrees construed an attack upon the principles of a civilized society—a disgrace to humanity! Life was hardly bearable, and melancholy permeated all. However, nobody had any clue of the ominous days yet to come. I felt like the Germans had constantly been sharpening their knives, with unlimited enthusiasm to slaughter us. We dreaded the days to come.

In March 1940, I was shoveling snow in front of our house. I did not take off my cap when a German policeman passed by, because I had not noticed him. "I am so sorry. I am just a little Jewish kid." I implored, but he mercilessly beat me. He could have killed me without any compunction. I was afraid to look at his face.

Whenever I saw the German *Hakenkreuz* (swastika, German for hooked cross), I was terrified. My stepmother told me that the swastika was widely used as an auspicious portent by Hindus and had been a symbol on Mesopotamian coins. In ancient times, it was considered as a symbol of prosperity and good fortune. *Swasti* means well-being. To me, it was a symbol of evil, and I hated it.

I had learned about the enslavement of Jews in Egypt, and that the Jews were oppressed by the Pharaohs, the Babylonians, the Persians, the Romans, and the Spanish government during the Spanish Inquisition, the Russian Czars, and the Khmelnitsky Cossacks, etc. The Jews have suffered centuries of concerted persecution. However, with all this information, I found that there was absolutely no comparison between those aforementioned atrocities, and the ones I have personally seen and endured under Adolph Hitler. The wanton cruelty we had to face brought us into a boundless despair. I could not understand why we always had the same obligations as other citizens but no rights to life, liberty and the pursuit of happiness as they had. Are not all human beings endowed with inalienable rights? I had committed no crime. I was not accused of any offense. I became a victim only by the accident of birth.

The Germans forcefully enlisted young Jews to work for enterprises that served the German war machine. In 1941, at the age of fourteen, I was assigned to a unit of the *Oberschleische Gumi Werke,* which operated in Chrzanów. I performed various manual chores; shelving materials, rendering parts, and cleaning, etc. I received no pay for my work. I have been receiving *Regelaltersrente,* a monthly pension since June 1998, for my uncompensated work in 1941.

In June 1941, in the dead of night, thundering Nazis knocked at our door, yelling, "*aufmachen schnell*" (open quickly). They manhandled my brother, Shmuel. He had hardly managed to pick up several personal belongings before he was grabbed away. We had no idea where he was going or for how long. From that moment, we did not hear from him.

In July 1941, I saw huge convoys of German vehicles with the signs, "*Nach Osten*" (to the east.). The previously invincible Red Army crumbled under the onslaught of Hitler's armies. The Germans were emboldened by their successes on all battlefronts, and they did not care about the opinion of the world. There were no signs that our misery would somehow be assuaged. The mass murder of Jews began in June 1941, and continued until the end of the war, in May 1945.

In January 1942, all Jewish residents in Chrzanów were ordered to surrender their furs and their jewelry to the *Judenrat* (Jewish Committee). The collected plunder was later delivered to the Germans. The Nazis achieved Jewish leaders' collaboration by threats and deceitful promises. The Jewish committees were thus forced to help in the registration, assembly, and eventual deportation of the Jewish community. Any dissent would be squelched. The Germans desperately needed winter clothing and woolens for their soldiers, who were exposed to harsh winter on the Russian battlefronts. They could not have cared less that Jews in Chrzanów were also freezing.

I was not aware when a neighbor took this picture on November 1, 1941. It reflects a fifteen-year-old boy in distress. I was wearing the Star of David armband. I worried about the new ominous Nazis' decrees I had to face.

This is the only prewar personal photo in my possession. Pepka Singer, a neighbor who survived the Holocaust, gave it to me. She managed to retain it during her captivity.

In February 1942, Betsalel Cuker, Kalmen Teichler and Mendl Nussbaum, members of the *Judenrat*, were beaten and then sent to Auschwitz, where they soon were murdered. In March of that same year, the SS came to inspect all Jewish homes to see whether the German orders had been fully complied with. If any jewelry or woolens, even worn-out children's fur collars were found, the owners were taken to the police station and brutally beaten.

In May 1942, during a day of mayhem, the Germans hung seven Jews of the community for trumped-up charges. Yisrael Gershtner and his two sons, Favyl Weissberger, Yehoshua Spangelet, Yisrael Frish and one Jew whose name I do not recall. This was another gruesome scene I shall never forget. All Jewish residents were ordered to come to the "Hanging Place" on Krzyska Street to watch the execution of their fellow co-religionists. A German policeman drove a truck through our neighborhood announcing with a megaphone, the "happy" event. "Today, seven Jewish criminals will be hung; tomorrow one hundred, and after tomorrow, all the Jewish criminals will be annihilated." German civilians with their wives, girlfriends and some Poles flocked to see the spectacle. All dressed up for the "festive occasion." The nooses were fastened to seven trees. For two hours, the Jews, including myself, being aghast, had to stand by and watch an orchestrated terrifying spectacle. I felt as if I were on the precipice of death myself. While the Jewish community was horrified, the throng of German and some Polish spectators didn't recoil, but rather watched with delight. They were agog and shrieked with laughter.

On February 18, 1943, the Germans sealed the town and summoned all the remaining Jews of Chrzanów into its marketplace. All Jews were to be transferred for "resettlement." **Chrzanów became** *Judenrein* **(free of Jews)**.

DEPORTATION

In June 1942, in the middle of the night, Nazis barged into our home. A young soldier with a smug smile shouted at me, *"Du knabe* (youngster), come with us. You have five minutes to get ready." I remember my eight-year-old brother crying, and clinging to his mother's apron. She momentarily held me close and sobbingly said, "I love you so much, my good soul."

My stepmother, Rachel, was panic-stricken and pleaded with the abductors, saying, "He is only fifteen. Please leave him with his mother. He needs her." One German soldier, with mirthless eyes and an aggressive face, was infuriated by her entreaty. He said, "How dare you to question our actions. Don't pretend to be courageous!" She was courageous, and she had always been. The SS man could have been chivalrous and let me stay. Instead, he yelled and struck my stepmother in her face. He knocked her down and she lost consciousness. The merciless villain was grinning; for he had no compunction. I was too stunned to say anything. I have been carrying an inconsolable grief in my heart because I never got a chance to say good-bye to my stepmother, and to my younger brother. Rachel's pleading words with the kidnappers were the last words that I remember her saying.

I was pulled out from my safe nest, and rammed down the stairs into the street where many despairing young Jews had already been assembled. Anxiety was gnawing a hole through my stomach. We were not handcuffed, but we were shoved into a police van. Then we were whipped like a herd of beasts. The Germans dragged us towards the local railroad station. We were taken to Sosnowiec, about thirty miles from home. In Sosnowiec, we were stuffed into an empty building for the night. We slept on the floor with empty stomachs. The following morning we boarded a truck, together with other Sosnowiec captives, and taken to the rail station. From there, we were transported to an undisclosed destination. About eighty men of different ages were loaded into one cattle car without food or water, and without any sanitary facilities. When one captive died, he remained standing because there was no room for him to fall. This was a hellish train.

FORCED LABOR AND CONCENTRATION CAMPS

BLECHHAMMER — ZWANGSARBEITSLAGER FÜR JUDEN,ZAL (FORCED LABOR CAMP FOR JEWS).

After an arduous journey, we arrived in *Blechhammer*, Upper Silesia, Germany, which is about forty-seven miles from Auschwitz. I was hungry, thirsty, soiled, and jaded. Upon arrival, a guard "welcomed" me with a blow in my face because it seemed to him that I did not move fast enough. I was terribly frightened! I begged the guard for water to quench my thirst, but he rendered blows to quench his beastly urges.

The newly constructed camp had a high barbed-wired fence. Machine-guns from watchtowers were pointed at 1,500 Jewish deportees from Chrzanów and its vicinity. There were no paved paths in that place—no trees, no meadows, and not a single blade of grass— just gravel and rocks between rows of wooden barracks.

MY BROTHER SHMUEL IS ALIVE!

On my second day in Blechhammer, an inmate whom I knew from Chrzanów asked me, "Do you know that your brother Shmuel is here?" I was surprised and delighted to find my brother. He had aged several years in the space of one, far removed from the fit figure I knew previously. Both of us were pleased to be together again. However, while my brother inured himself to his fate, he was very apprehensive as to whether I, at such a tender age, could endure the brutalizing conditions that he already had experienced during one year of captivity.

THE BUNKS WE SLEPT ON

In Blechhammer, I was allotted the middle narrow plank of a three-level bunk. This was not as bad as in some infamous death camps, like Auschwitz, where five people were crammed together onto one small bed, a meter wide. There was no mattress, no bed sheet and no pillows—just straw and a coarse blanket. Eight such bunks, holding twenty-four men, were crammed into an 8' x 10' room in a wooden barrack. Nobody could have any privacy other than in his own thoughts.

It was a motley group of people, ranging in age from sixteen to sixty. There were rich and poor, religious and secular, erudite and ignorant, wise and foolish, prominent and plebeian, obsessive and idiosyncratic, and easy-going and easily annoyed. There were merchants, poor artisans, and pupils, like myself. We were all facing torture, starvation, and probable death—not simply dying, but dying in humiliation.

In the evenings, there were often roll calls that lasted for hours. We were forced to stand outside, sometimes in freezing weather or rain. Eventually, we went to sleep exhausted. Anxieties kept us awake at night. When the darkness of the night ended, the darkness of the day's travails began.

There was no room, and no spare time for intellectual camaraderie. The atmosphere was suffused with a feeling of helplessness. Nobody was in the mood to even tell or listen to a funny joke. Entertainers and pranksters kept silent; the general mood would not have been receptive. There was no time to meditate or cogitate. There was hardly anybody with whom to commiserate. I felt like a loner among loners. Mahatma Gandhi said, "Where there is love, there is life." There was none in the camp. My mind focused on surviving the day. I had no philosophical musings on a lasting life. I lived in perpetual dread, and I had nobody to push my fears away. The prevailing brutality suffocated our intelligence and our critical faculties. It was hard to make a friend or find an old friend who would be able or willing to listen to my emotional cries and physical pains. We all retreated into ourselves. A smile, which is usually so easy to pass along, never did surface. I faced silhouettes of contorted faces staring at the shadow of death. The prevalence of despair never fluctuated. Murderous actions took place everyday. There was nothing in the air to inject even false hopes.

Withering heat in summer and severe freezing coldness in winter exacerbated the depressive atmosphere in the barracks. The bunks also served as the inmate's dining table. There was no other designated area for eating.

I witnessed the agony of the man on the bunk above me, dying from starvation. This was the first victim dying in front of my eyes. I saw many more dead and dying victims in Blechhammer, and in the other camps during my captivity. I became prey to fears of my own survival.

HYGIENE

There was a small *badnezimmer* (bathroom) consisting of several shower stalls and a few washbasins to clean ourselves and wash our clothes. It was obviously inadequate to accommodate 1,500 men. We all strove to get into that bathroom. We were dirty and so were our clothes. This was just one component of daily hardship. There were no flushing toilets—just one large outhouse with holes to accommodate many, without any privacy. Inmates had to stand in long lines just to relieve themselves. No toilet paper or any other kind of disposable wipes were provided. At night, no one was permitted to go outside. Therefore, a bucket served as a latrine. If its content overflowed, the *Kapos* struck us indiscriminately with whips and sticks. Our filthy clothes were infested with lice.

We were, ironically, expected to practice personal hygiene under the most unhygienic and unsanitary conditions. Most inmates had an offensive breath stemming from hunger, untreated infections, chemical imbalance, and lack of minerals/vitamins. We had no toothbrush or dental floss to clean our teeth.

KAPOS

The German commander selected *funktionien* (functionaries)—prisoners to help the Germans carry out many of the daily affairs in the camp. We had a *Lagerältester* (camp senior) who served like an interlocutor and a *blockältester* (barrack senior). There were *Kapos* (inmate bosses) or overseers who could give orders and hurt us with immunity. Those inmate-supervisors were given the power of life or death over the rest of us who were under their control. Most of those chosen were bad people, of a devious character. Some were demons, outcasts in the communities they came from. They carried hard rubber truncheons and used them at their discretion, sometimes with much cruelty. They beat and bullied us in the camp, on the march to and from work, and at the workplace. They never talked to us. They just shouted at us in agitated voices. I feared them as I feared the German guards. The flogging by a Kapo was as painful as the flogging by a German.

FOOD

One inmate from each room was selected to be *Stubeneltester* (room senior). His assignment in the early morning was to pick up the rounded loaves of bread, black *ersatz* (substitute) coffee and whatever else from the camp's pantry to be distributed among the inmates of his room. He cut the small rounded loaves in eight segments, so we each received one-eighth of a loaf and a morsel of margarine, marmalade, or whatever else was on the menu for that day. Sometimes there was nothing else but the bread. Sawdust was one ingredient of the bread. Most people, under normal circumstances, would consider the bread to be inedible. We had no other choice. Any plea to alleviate our predicament would have had the same effect as sticking a fist into a bucket of water. Abuse and torture was a constant on the daily menu. I envied the Germans' well-fed dogs.

That bread ration was for breakfast and lunch. It had always left me with a dilemma. Should I eat the bread right away or keep it for later, at the working place? In the evening, after we returned from work, we were jostling in line in front of the camps' kitchen to get our bowl of soup. The diluted soup had floating potatoes or peels from the potatoes, other vegetables, and slices of meat (occasionally horse meat).

OTHER GROUPS OF INMATES

On the way to our working place, we noticed other marching groups of prisoners—British POWs, Russian POWs, Czechs, German communists, German deserters, wayward German citizens, gypsies, Poles, Serbs Ukrainian, AEL *Arbeitserziehungslger* (Work Education Camp), *Politische haeftlinge* (political prisoners) *Bibelforscher*, (Jehovah's Witnesses) *Homoexuelle*, (homosexuals), and many others. In all, there were perhaps twenty to thirty groups from different nations. Each group was housed in a separate camp. Most faces of the marching prisoners were ashen and fear-ridden. They were dragging their feet. Every prisoner wore a distinguishing triangle or badge. Criminals wore green triangles, political prisoners wore red ones, homosexuals wore pink ones, Jehovah's Witnesses wore lavender ones, and Jews wore a yellow Star of David.

Apparently, all those captives were deemed by the Germans to be *untermentchen* (subhuman). Many times, we could see how those marching men were beaten, sometimes to death by their guards. In Blechhammer, I became aware that Jews were not the only victims. **Every Jew was a victim, but not all victims were Jews. This was not a mere manifestation of anti-Semitism; it was a manifestation of anti-humanism.**

WORK

We worked six days a week and sometimes even on Sundays. A *Kapo* woke us up early in the morning. We were ordered to assemble at the *Appellplatz*, (gathering place) and be standing for half an hour or longer, even in inclement weather. The *Kapos*, in presence of the camp's commandant, conducted the *Zeil Appel* (head count). Those who were missing at the *Zeil Appel* had died from starvation, exposure, work accidents, or were brutally slain by the guards on the previous day.

We were escorted to work by the *Kapos* and German guards who sometimes unleashed their dogs on the inmates, especially those who could not keep up with the marching pace. The dogs were barking and so did the guards. Most guards were drawn into Hitler's orbit of brutality due to blind obedience and fear. Not all German guards marched in lockstep with their demonic colleagues. Some were not driven by blood lust, and they carried out their duty of guarding us without using excessive force. All guards were clean-shaven and meticulously dressed. The guards' pleasant appearance did not reflect their characters. You could see a clean pot on the outside, but if the inside was dirty, it would still poison you. Some guards were goons or just slouchy old men who, under normal circumstances, would have lived in cozy facilities for the semi-retired rather than guarding us in frequently rough weather. They were too frail to bully us. Other guards revealed blatant coolness. None of the guards acted affably, though they might have been affable. The wicked far outnumbered the virtuous.

I do not recall that anybody managed to escape or considered escaping as a feasible option while trudging to work—either from the working place or from the camp site. Had one of us managed to escape, all the other prisoners would have been collectively punished. We were birds with broken wings. There would be no assurance of freedom for any escapee in such a hostile environment that surrounded us. We were asphyxiated.

Our body strength was utilized to build a titanic synthetic gasoline plant for *Oberschlesische Hydrierwerke AG.* It was supposedly going to be the largest such plant in the world. Some of our inmates were employed, rather enslaved, by various concerns for the construction of factories, building roads, underground warehouses, and air raid bunkers. In many instances, we were abused by being used as substitutes for bulldozers, cranes, and jackhammers, etc. In other instances, we were forced into a boondoggle—another way for humiliation.

During the first few weeks in Blechhammer, I worked to prepare the grounds for construction. Cut trees were removed by carrying them on our shoulders.

Some inmates succumbed while lifting large logs. Fallen inmates, who had been beaten to death or expired at work, were also removed, and carried on our shoulders, sometimes on stretchers, back to the camp.

We worked long hours, sometimes ten hours or more. We had one short break but most often, we were not given any food. Inmates who managed to retain the morning portion of bread ate it at break time. We were worked to death and often beaten by the guards, *Kapos,* and also by the supervisors of the German companies. Any German could hurt us at will; they had carte blanche to do so. I was told that I.G. Farben had some control over my work. This is the company that twenty-three of its officials were put on trial in 1947. Thirteen defendants were convicted for war crimes, including plunder and the use of slave labor. Many supervisors, who were employees of the company we worked for, were quite mean. They used and abused our strength. They sucked our blood during the day and the lice sucked our blood at night. The lice and cockroaches flourished in the filthy straw that we had to sleep on while we were fading away. Once, I stumbled and dropped the log

I was carrying on my shoulder. The foreman screamed at me, saying, "You are a worthless horse in my stable!" He seemed to be wishing to snap my cord of life. He could have done so with impunity. At work, or marching to and from work, we had no shelter from inclement weather. We were at all times vulnerable and doomed. I remember when one of the inmates who was badly beaten howled and pleaded with the Germans, "Please kill me," but the German supervisor refused because he enjoyed watching the man suffer.

While at work, we had to ask *Erlaubnis* (permission to relieve ourselves). There were no lavatories—just holes in the ground. There was no privacy other than the shadow of a bush or scrub. We could not navigate by our own compass.

MY WRISTWATCH FOR A LOAF OF BREAD

Some of us who worked closely with prisoners from other groups could communicate if there was no language barrier. The very first week in Blechhammer, a Pole had noticed that I was wearing a wristwatch. At that point, I still had my clothes, family photos, and a few personal belongings that I had brought with me from home. The Pole said to me. "I see you have a watch. If you give me your watch, tomorrow I will bring you a loaf of bread." I was naïve and desperately hungry, so I gave him my watch. I trusted that he would deliver the promised loaf of bread.

Coming back from work that same day, all the inmates were called to assemble at the *Appellplatz* for announcements. The evil camp commandant, carrying a riding whip, said, "Today, one of you gave away his wristwatch to a Pole for a promised loaf of bread. As you know, this is an infraction of our rules, and if that *häftling* (detainee) does not step forward to admit his crime, all of you will be punished. You will not rest, but will stand here the entire night and march to work tomorrow morning, like any other day."

I stepped forward and with a trembling voice I said "I am the one who gave my watch to a Pole who promised to give me a loaf of bread, because I am so hungry. I know that my brother is hungry, too!" The commandant dismissed all the other prisoners back to their barracks. My legs were trembling as he summoned me to his post. The commandant with a scowling expression whipped me in my face and ordered the *Kapos* to take me to the "punishment room" which was very notorious. Every molecule in my body was shaking. I was ordered to take off all my clothes. A *Kapo*, with a leather thong, flogged fifteen lashes on my bare back. Two German guards made sure that I received minimum compassion and maximum pain.

Most prisoners who got dragged to that room did not come out alive. I was within an inch of my life, but somehow, perhaps miraculously, I did survive that ordeal. I recited the *Birchat Hagomeil* (The Benediction of Deliverance). My brother was waiting for me nearby. When he saw me in excruciating pain, he broke down. My mind was blank. I could hardly walk. I felt sore with bruises all over my body. My skin was ripped open in several spots. I was bleeding and crying. I lost the little strength that I had left and my thirst for life. No doctors or nurses were called to help me. My brother and two of his roommates dragged me to my bunk. He was glad to see me alive, and with pride he told my roommates, " *Zeh nes myn hashamayim*" (This is a miracle from heaven). You should all be grateful to Alter for admitting that he was the one and thus nobody else was punished but him. Our father taught us that everybody should be responsible for his own actions, and Alter abided by our father's teachings."

In October 1942, I was sent to another camp called Brande. My brother continued to stay in Blechhammer, but I do not know for how long. We were separated on my sixteenth birthday. The sky was dark and gray. I was shivering from cold weather and blatant fear. I asked the officer to let me stay with my older brother. He simply clobbered me. My fear was that if we were separated, we would not see each other again. Indeed, I have not seen my brother since.

Out of my twenty-four roommates in Blechhammer, only Motle Engle and I survived the Holocaust. The rest apparently were crushed to dust under the Nazi's killing apparatus.

The camp was liberated by the Soviet Army on January 28, 1945. Blechhammer became part of Poland and is known today as Blachownia Slaska.

BRANDE — ZWANGSABEITSLAGER FÜR JUDEN, ZAL (FORCED LABOR CAMP FOR JEWS)

Brande was a small camp for about 800 Jews. The living quarters, the filthy latrines, the scarcity of food and all other horrendous conditions were about the same as those in Blechhammer. Apparently, Blechammer was a template for other camps designated for Jews. However, here, the commander, with roughly chiseled features and a booming voice, was much crueler. Hatred oozed out of him at every pore. His appearance, with a whip under his arm, made chills run up my back. I felt that he was going to do me in. The barracks were riddled with termites. It was a very harsh winter, sometimes subzero temperatures, and we had no warm clothes. Some of us died of exposure.

Our group helped to build the *Reichsautobahn* (the major highway) which was designed to run across Germany. We had to trudge to and from the working site for several miles. I suffered from frostbite (two of my toes have never completely healed). My shoes from home were completely worn out, and were replaced by clogs, which had wooden soles, and the upper part was made of a coarse fabric. The snow stuck to the soles, and the walk became very difficult. We were afraid to trip, because the guards would hit us as surely as a hammer would smash an eggshell. When one of us did stumble, the guards beat the fallen person, sometimes to death. We had no gloves. The fingers of many inmates froze. Some died of hypothermia.

I was deported to a forced labor camp, rather than to a death camp, to have my strength utilized for the German war effort as long as possible. It was reminiscent of Pharaoh of Egypt who kept the Hebrews as slaves, to help build the pyramids. The squalor and suffering in Brande where I was in servitude were so lethal that many succumbed shortly after their arrival. It seemed that those forced labor camps were established for the purpose of extermination through labor, rather than to keep the German economy abreast. The Germans would rather abuse us than use us as substitutes for the German workforce, which had been mobilized for military services. The Germans had a reputation of being superbly efficient. While thousands of skilled working Jewish men were annihilated, the ministries of industry of the German Reich were in constant search for evermore manpower. This was a paradoxical phenomenon that I did not understand. Apparently, the Germans were no prudent slave owners. They had an asinine policy! Nazi Germany was rushing to develop the apparatus of death rather than spur the economy.

Short in manpower, Hitler ordered thousands of common criminals to be released from jail. He thrust them into positions of authority where they could vent their personal frustrations on the captives subjugated to their whim. They were assigned to positions of power. It reminds me of how Saddam Hussein of Iraq let out 150,000 common criminals, before the second Gulf War started in February 2003.

That commandant was a sadist. His contempt for us manifested by using foul language and curses to belittle us. He amused himself by torturing us. I never knew his name, but I do remember his square jaw and cruel smile. He pushed me and other inmates under a frigid shower in an unheated washroom and left us standing there for the entire night. I still remember the yelling, the inflicted pain, the offensive smell, the dirt, and the taste of sweat in that washroom. I am not able to forget that commandant's loathsome brutality. While he basked in the glory of German military victories, we were made to shiver and die under cold showers. Several of us did die; the washroom became a venue for bloodbaths.

We were often subjected to prolonged exposure to cold. This cruel commander's appetite for torturing his victims was insatiable. He was a criminal who had stepped outside the bounds of civilization. He wore a prosthetic leg due to an injury he had sustained during his pre-war criminal activities. The sound of his voice nauseated me. I do not know if the bestiality that came over him was because he was complying with Hitler's orders, or because he was just a beast in a human frame. In either case, I wondered how he could live for the rest of his life with the load of suffering he had brought to so many innocent people.

On the other hand, one day, a German guard who appeared to be tough as nails, threw a little brown bag at me which had one slice of bread in it. A good person may be found among the wicked, and looks sometimes do not always profile the person.

After two months, I was transferred to another camp called Gross Masselwitz. I do not think that I could have lasted longer in that ephemeral hell, called Brande.

LIBERATION

Brande was dissolved in December 1943, and the surviving prisoners were transferred to other camps. After the war, I read that the chronically ill among the inmates in Brande had benzene injected into their bloodstream. The victims were seized by convulsions that chocked them to death after a while. This poison did not let them die in comfort. The area of Brande was liberated in January 1945 by the Russian Army. It became part of Poland after the war, and the name changed to Prądy.

GROSS MASSELWITZ — ZAL
ZWANGSABEITSLAGER FÜR JUDEN

I arrived in December 1942 to a camp where about 1,500 Jews were crammed into a large warehouse. The living conditions and food rations were similar to the previous two camps. However, we had to endure less hardship because the commander did not act as brutally as the two previous commanders in Brande and Blechhammer did. Also, we did not have to march so many miles to our working place.

One of the inmates, Simcha Schonberg, said to me, "I would like to be your mentor, to help you as much as I can. I was lying next to your father when the German shot him and me. I am the one who managed to escape during the night by pretending to be dead." In practical terms, there was not much that Mr. Schonberg could have done to help me. He just had sympathy for me because of my tender age.

I worked in military warehouses above and below the ground, not far from our camp. When we saw those huge warehouses stockpiled with heavy weapons and military supplies, even the optimists among us doubted whether the Germans would ever be defeated. It was irritating that we were actually helping the Germans to build their mighty fortresses. Our hope for deliverance diminished. While the Germans were in an aura of triumph, we lived in an aura of helplessness.

The German efficiency warranted admiration. Any item collected on the battlefront, such as uniforms of German casualties or enemies, their personal belongings, and their guns, reached Gross Masselwitz's rail terminal. We had to unload the train cars, assort, repair, clean, and shelve all those items in warehouses.

While unloading a train car, a machine gun fell on my foot. I was groaning and writhing in pain. I felt like I was bleeding and wanted to take off my clog to see what had happened. Perhaps I could find some kind of an improvised bandage with which to bind my toe. The guard did not permit me. I had to continue to work. Coming back to camp in the evening, I realized that my toe was badly injured, and my nail was loose. I was in constant pain for a long time. That toe has never completely healed.

A RIGHTEOUS GERMAN

In July 1943, the Germans selected a building of a textile factory to be re-equipped for the production of armaments and ammunition. Being competent and efficient as they were, the Germans let the employees (mostly German females) continue to operate their textile machinery in one section of the factory, while we inmates were stationed in another part of that factory dismantling old machines and putting up new ones.

There were signs all over the factory warning the German employees not to communicate with the *häftlinge* (detainees) or even make eye contact with them. Anyone who did not comply with those rules would be *Verdammnt* (doomed!).

One day a middle-aged, dark-haired German woman, on the way to the restroom, did make eye contact with me, and pointed her finger at a box. I was very curious but had to watch myself so that neither a guard nor another inmate would notice me approaching that box. At the proper moment, I managed to reach that box and I found a sandwich underneath it. I went to the lavatory designated for prisoners, and devoured the sandwich, in haste. The sandwich consisted of two slices of white bread with a slice of cheese. It was a beautiful day and suddenly I wanted so much to stay alive. Not only did I feel stronger physically, but also my faith in humanity strengthened.

That lady repeated that noble act of leaving a sandwich for me every day, for as long as I worked in that building. Those sandwiches might have helped me to survive! I have no yardstick to measure that. It was only for thirty days out of 1,050 days of my captivity. However, I do know that her righteous deed gave me hope. She was a glowing candle in a silver candlestick jutting out in the darkness, while my candle of life was melting to the point of wax residue.

The pivotal question has been what motivated that German woman to risk her life for me, a stranger? I was only a young Jewish boy—an *untermentch* (a subhuman) by Nazi criterion. She ignored the daily-propagandized odium and helped me. So many people were killing each other and she was willing to die for me? Why? Did she have a son at my age and felt sorry for me? Was she a religious person who tried to abide by the tenets of her faith, by succoring the helpless? Did she follow the dictates of her conscience, motivated by her goodness? Was her intention to manifest that not all Germans were inhumane? Did she wish to assert that under the most ruthless dictatorship, a single human conscience could fight back? Did she want to patch up a punctured veneer of civilization, telling me and to herself that we both were cut from the same human cloth? I would like very much to know her motive but, regretfully, I shall never know! Unlike angels that have to follow divine instructions, that righteous German lady followed the dictates of her free will, which is a God-given gift.

Her extended hand led me to believe that I had no justification to hate each and every German for murdering hundreds of close and distant relatives of mine, as well as millions of others. It would be unjust for me to slap a noxious label on the entire German nation. There are good and evil people in each ethnicity. Not all Germans had a common moral depravity embedded in their culture. Some Germans did not let themselves be manipulated or hypnotized by the Nazi propaganda! I recognize that there were indeed Germans who had refused to commit atrocities. There were German leaders, like Willy Brandt (German Chancellor in 1969) who had chosen exile in order to fight the ideology of his native land's leader. It would be unfair to put all Germans on trial.

The sharp contrast between the conduct of the nefarious guard who knocked out my teeth several months earlier—mentioned in my Preface—and the righteous woman who gave me the sandwiches, both German nationals, is a compelling affirmation that good and evil dwell in each ethnic group. She was the antidote of the venal and incurably violent side of Nazi Germany. She tickled my imagination and my dream of a caring world.

Experiencing the abhorrent behavior of so many Germans, I got the impression that there was something congenitally malevolent about the German people. I assumed that no German was immune from not committing atrocities. However, that German lady who had risked her life for me stands out in my memory. She helped to shape my philosophical evolution, and the way I act and interact to this very day. I realized then that it would be unfair to accuse the entire German people of complicity to commit genocide of the "inferiors." It is due, in part, to that German noble lady that I chose not to judge people based on their nationality, race, ethnicity or religion. She prevents me from stereotypical thinking.

The Bible tells us in Genesis 18:23, "Will you sweep away the righteous and the wicked, the innocent and the guilty?" If there is one righteous person in a village where everybody else is wicked, the entire village must not be destroyed! By the same token, I shall not hate the German people as a people because of that noble German woman. It has become a major guiding light in the path of my life. That unidentified German woman jeopardized her life to alleviate my despondency and my hunger pangs. I shall forever remember her daring act. She had the conviction and the courage to risk her own life to save another's life—to save someone so very different from herself. She has been, and forever will be, my heroine.

> *"True heroism is not dramatic. It is not the urge to surpass all others at whatever cost, but the urge to serve others at whatever cost."*
> —Arthur Ashe

I asked *Yad Vashem*, the Holocaust memorial in Jerusalem, Israel, to consider my heroine as one of the *Hasidei Ummot Ha-olam* (Righteous among Nations) to have a tree planted in the "Alley of the Righteous." Perhaps she would not be interested in receiving public recognition for her noble act, but I felt it was my duty to recognize her. My request was declined for the obvious reason that I could not provide a name and address of the person whom I recommended to be honored. Nevertheless, I believe that my heroine's righteous deeds merit her to be among the righteous, such as, Raoul Wallenberg, the Swedish diplomat who acted with great courage and dignity to save thousands of Hungarian Jews; Oscar Schindler, who saved 1,100 Jews; Sugihara, the Japanese diplomat, who saved thousands of Lithuanian Jews; Dr Feng Shan Ho, Chinese Consul General in Vienna, who issued exit visas to thousands of Jewish families in Austria, Hiram Bingham IV, the American vice consul in Marseilles for his role in rescuing Jews from the south of France during 1940-1941, Corrie ten Boom, who saved Jews in the Netherlands, and many other rescuers and saviors.

There are many righteous people whose names we shall never know, who lost their lives for helping to save the life of a prisoner like me.

In April 2006, Paul Spiegel, the leader of the Jewish Council in Germany, died. During the war, he was hidden in Belgium by a family of Christian farmers. After the war, he returned to Germany. When he found out that his father's neighbors had risked their lives to conceal and preserve sacred text from the local synagogues, he decided to stay in Germany. Most of his family members perished in the Holocaust, but the righteousness of his father's German neighbors convinced him that Germany was still his home. My German heroine gave me the impetus not to paint all Germans with the same brush.

I bow my head for all righteous people of all nations, who risked death to preserve human freedom and human dignity. We must honor them by carrying on their struggle to defend life, liberty, and justice for all people.

LIBERATION

The camp was dissolved in spring 1944. It became part of Poland. The Polish name for Gross-Masselwitz is Dzielnica Maślice Wielkie.

KLETENDORF — ZWANGSABEITSLAGER ZAL FÜR JUDEN

After fifteen months in Gross Masselwitz, I was transferred to Klettendorf. This was a camp of several hundred prisoners, and among them were Jews who had recently arrived from Western Europe. Those prosperous and highly educated Jews enjoyed a climate of tolerance which had started in the 17th century. They had not been exposed to the Anti-Semitic discrimination as many of their co-religionists in Eastern Europe had been. Coming from a comfortable environment to a forced labor camp was unbearable to them. Many soon flinched and succumbed.

A recent arrival from Belgium noticed me eating a raw potato, and he said to me in Yiddish, "How in the world can you eat a raw, dirty, and unpeeled potato? How can you take all this humiliation, beating, and starvation? You are being abased by evil fascists! Isn't it self-depreciating?" My response was, "I have been enslaved here, and slaves have no pride! If you would have experienced two-and-one-half years of camp life as I have, you probably would have done the same. When you are very hungry, day-in and day-out, and never sated, you, too, would be glad to find and eat a raw potato. I have been starving for a long time. I consider myself extremely lucky to have found a potato that a farmer had left in his field. It tasted better than my occasional foraging for peels of potatoes or chewing snow."

At that time, the Germans were losing battles on several fronts. We were digging trenches and putting up barriers against incoming tanks. The man said to me, "I was a precocious schoolboy. I had wonderful parents, a wife, and children. We had a thriving business and a rich cultural life. Without my family, I have no desire to live, and it is senseless to suffer from a psychopathic tyrant like Hitler and his cohorts. I would rather die! He did die two weeks after our conversation. This heart-wrenching episode I shall never forget.

A FREIGHT TRAIN WITH HUMAN CARGO

In Klettendorf, I had a horrifying glance at a long train of cattle cars, filled with guarded human cargo. It passed close to the trench that I was digging. I could hear moaning and pleading for *Wasser* (water). That train was heading towards one of the six extermination camps— **Auschwitz, Belzec, Chelmno, Maidanek, Sobibor and Treblinka,** located in occupied Poland. That horrifying spectacle still reverberates in my memory. I witnessed a nefarious design of human cruelty towards innocent people. Yet, I was unable to strangle the last sight of it. I was strangled by it.

The murder of the victims in that train continues to this very day, because those who could procreate were murdered.

I could not understand then, and I do not understand today, the logic to send non-combatants to death. Few of the perpetrators have ever been brought to trial, but the character of civilization was! How could such slaughter go on without arousing the civilized world's wrath?

That evening, back from work, I could not eat. The faces of the doomed, peeping out from the tiny windows of the boxcars were flitting before my eyes. Having watched genocide unfold has haunted me ever since. By that time, in August 1944, the democratic world undoubtedly was aware of the death camps in Poland and Germany. I wondered whether Jews in America were protesting the slaughter of their brethren. Why didn't the United States, a nation founded and populated by the oppressed of different faiths and from many lands, stop Hitler's genocide? Where were the good Samaritans among the American Christians? They were expected to have compassionate regard for all people, not just some people! Where were the fighters for human rights? How could their humanitarian reputations be maintained when our suffering became unbearable? I doubted if the faithful of religious denominations said a prayer for our deliverance! Their silence was spiritual poverty! Pope John Paul II referred to the Jewish People as "Our elder brothers in the faith." He also declared anti-Semitism to be a sin against God. Apparently, people of the world put up a wall to isolate themselves from seeing our suffering. Was everybody in the outside world a passive accomplice? Where were the human rights groups? Was it not a betrayal of basic human solidarity? Was it not a failure of the entire moral fabric of society? There was nothing that those inmates inside the camps could do to alleviate their situation. Help could only come from the outside world, but the outside world failed to respond. I believe now that even mass demonstrations in the democratic countries around the world would have forced the German to stop, or at least moderate their policy of *Ausrottung* (the extermination) of European Jewry. If President Roosevelt had been more vociferous in expressing his and the American people's indignation, the nonchalant world would have been awakened, and they would have protested the slaughter of the innocent.

In camps, we used to say, "We are treated like dogs." It would definitely not be applicable to the way dogs are treated today. The Atlanta zoo pays China $2 million a year for renting a pair of giant pandas. Those pandas consume eighty-four pounds of vegetables a day. Our life had no value. Apparently, if those cattle wagons were destined to killing centers, they would have carried dogs or horses, rather than Jewish children. There would have been a world outcry against cruelty to animals. How could civilization stomach such ongoing slaughter of the innocent? That was unconscionable! After the Liberation, I learned that as far back as November 1942, the public in the U.S. and around the world had reliable information about the systematic extermination of European Jewry, but the news media displayed a monumental disinterest in our ordeal, and hence let evil triumph.

It was, and it still is, a painful feeling of being abandoned by the international community. Had it not been so indifferent, the Genocide (the term was coined in 1944) could have been stopped, or at least interrupted, to not allow the dikes of civilization to collapse. The widespread oppression didn't always happen in hidden places. The camps were large enough to be seen through the lenses of the contemporary cameras in the possession of the Allies' intelligence. Somehow, I believed that God was watching the indifference of the world, and that God himself was brokenhearted as well.

LIBERATION

Klettendorf was dissolved in the late autumn of 1944. It has become part of Poland. The Polish name for Klettendorf is Klecina.

WALDENBURG — KONZENTRATIONSLAGER-KL (CONCENTRATION CAMP)

In September 1944, I was transferred from Klettendorf to a *Konzentrationslager-KL* (concentration camp) in Waldenburg, (concentration camp is a term coined by the Germans to describe camps for the enemy detainees who were kept in the German colonies of southwest Africa at the beginning of the 20th century). Waldenburg was a recently constructed camp which consisted of several three-story buildings. Many new, small and large, camps were quickly built to accommodate the constant flow of new political and non-political prisoners. Our camp was located in a desolate mountainous area. Flowers, meadows, and residential homes were not part of the landscape—no lakes or brooks—just an occasional stream of the inmates' blood. It was dreadful scenery without solace. I do not recall seeing a female or a child around the camp or at the working place. It felt like I was abandoned in a desert with nothing but the edge of a knife to keep me company. About 600 Jewish prisoners were incarcerated in Waldenburg. It was an oppressive and depressive environment. We were no longer guarded by the Wehrmacht soldiers but by the SS.*Schutzstaffel*, Protection Squad.

Upon arrival, we were ordered to take off all our clothes. Demonic characters stripped us of everything we possessed including our dignity. I noticed several German guards putting some inmates' valuables into their pockets. They preferred to enrich themselves rather than Germany's Treasury Dept. Their greed was unbridled by Nazi ideology.

I was given a shirt, a crude prison uniform with blue stripes, and a round striped cap, an overcoat and a pair of wooden clogs. We got neither underwear, nor socks. There were no pockets in our uniforms. We were left without any personal possessions other than a shallow metallic bowl with a spoon.

FROM A NAME TO A NUMBER

At that juncture, my first and last name was replaced by a number. My number, **64735,** was attached to the cap, to the jacket and to the overcoat. I became nameless and faceless because there were no mirrors.

To make us easily recognizable, in case one tried to escape, a narrow strip of hair was shaved from our heads. The Germans called it the *Lause Strasse* (the street of the lice). Occasionally, we could shower in cold water, in a chilly bathroom. The Germans called it *Entlausung* (ridding of lice).

Most of us were working for a construction company that built underground military warehouses. In March 1945, we heard a massive explosion that shook buildings, sending chunks of plaster and concrete close to where we were working. The air filled with smoke. Then we heard a second deafening explosion. We didn't see airplanes dropping bombs. However, our wishful thinking was that the enemies of Germany were hitting our tormentors.

SUICIDAL NOTION

In February 1945, I was very weak, in despair and despondent. I wished to die to put an end to my suffering. I said to myself, "I cannot go to hell from here because there cannot be a hell worse than the one I was in." I felt that it had become senseless to decay like that. Why stay alive while so many lives had been destroyed? I had a strong desire to touch something beautiful before I died, like a flower, but here was none in my surroundings. It was forbidden to approach the electric fence surrounding the camp. My intent was to touch that fence and be electrocuted. I was thinking, if I am beaten to death or starved to death, it would not matter because I was literally dead already. Furthermore, I thought that I would be reunited with my parents in heaven. However, I hesitated as I recalled a phrase in the prayer book which read, "God in heaven decides whether a person should live or die." I was clinging to the last tissue—thin strands of hope. The suffering infused me with hope for messianic redemption. The suicidal feelings stayed with me for a long time, but my strong roots of faith did not let my tree of life fall.

CREMATORIUM

Our strength was utilized to serve the Germans might, and when we could no longer work due to sickness or emaciation, we were destined to be transferred to a death camp to be murdered and cremated.

By March 1945, I was so emaciated that I could no longer work, and I became a candidate for liquidation—thus, one less mouth to feed. The Nazis had a very utilitarian concept—the more inferior and unproductive people they could eliminate, the better off the Arian race would be. There was no shortage of barbarity in Waldenburg, but it had no gas chambers. So, I was transferred to a camp (I do not remember the name) where a crematorium did exist. For me, the image of that place will last for eternity. The *Kapos* informed us that we were due for disinfection and cleansing. I learned later that those victims of that disinfection process were ushered into gas chambers. In some cases, organs were removed from the victims for further medical research. Gold dental work was removed and sent to the German Central Bank. Clothes were recycled. Jewelry, toys, spectacles, and even skin and hair of the dead were utilized to serve the German economy.

DESTRUCTION THROUGH WORK

I was standing in line for the doomed, waiting to be gased and cremated. I sniffed the offensive odor of burning flesh. I felt downright scared. The thought of being so close to an imminent death sucked the life out of me. I "consoled" myself with the thought that if so many wonderful people were being murdered, what difference would my death make? Then, a German civilian entrepreneur approached me. My heart stopped. He shouted at me, " *Komm raus, Knabe, du kannst doch bei der Arbeit krepieren"* (get out of the line, young boy; you can still work and expire at work). He sent me back to Waldenburg. This was in line with the Nazi's plan *Vernichtung durch Arbeit*, (destruction through work). In other words, I was sentenced to death on the first day of incarceration, but I was forced to work until the day of extermination.

LIBERATION

We were liberated by the Russian Army. Waldenburg became part of Poland; and was renamed Wałbrzych.

LIBERATION FROM NAZI YOKE AND THE ENSUING ODYSSEY

NAZI GUARDS DISAPPEARED AND THE RUSSIAN LIBERATORS ARRIVED

On May 9, 1945, we assembled at the regular *"Zeil Appel."* We were standing at *Achtung* (motionless) until about 10.00 a.m., waiting to be counted and marched to work. No guards showed up. Even the omnipresent guards on the watchtowers who were permeating our camp disappeared. About that time, somebody threw the key of the main gate and told us that we would be free soon. We were all apprehensive wondering if that was an ominous trick.

We had been cut off from any source of information. We had no calendars, no newspapers, and no radio. We were skeptical that the war might have come to an end, because we deemed the Germans to be invincible. We did not hear any sounds of battle and wondered if it was all a trap. There had recently been a rumor in our camp that a "good" German guard surreptitiously confided to an inmate that Germany was losing the war. Still, it was unimaginable that we should ever be granted a new life.

THE RUSSIAN LIBERATORS

A Russian tank approached the gate of our camp. An officer stepped out from his tank and told us, "We have come to liberate you!" We couldn't understand his Russian language, but we obviously understood that Germany had indeed been defeated. A flurry of excitement enveloped the camp but I do not recall an outburst of jubilation among the inmates. We were in a daze. Like Moses, a Russian colonel appeared to deliver the Jews from slavery. He announced, to our surprise, in halting Yiddish, "*Yidden ihr zent frai* (**Jews you are free**)!" We are giving you three days of absolute freedom to rape, to steal and even to kill Germans who tortured you. We have full empathy for your suffering, because we have lost 22 million of our people, and tens of thousands of our villages and towns were wiped out."

The officer fervently derided the Nazis. Some of our liberators were vengeful. Many Germans expressed shock and annoyance at the opprobrium the Russians caused. I did not go out to kill and rape because I was too weak to do anything. Furthermore, had I been well, I could not have hurt anybody. It was just not ingrained in me. I remembered my father's slogan, "Hate hatred, and shun violence!" I also recalled from Leviticus (19:18),"You shall not take vengeance or bear a grudge." I was definitely not vengeful! I was grateful that the Germans did not succeed during the Holocaust in debasing my inherited values which were instilled in me during the formative years of my life. The Nazis damaged my constitution but could not break it.

When Solomon became king of the Israelites, God told him to ask for what he wanted, and he would grant it (Kings 3:5, 7-12). Solomon asked for an understanding heart, to know how to distinguish right from wrong. When I became a liberated man, I asked God to enable me to live in a peaceful world among the righteous and not to have to face the wicked again.

The Russian officer broke down and wept while glancing at our emaciated bodies. I remember tears rolling down the faces of many brave Russian soldiers while staring at us—dejected skeletons—the results of Hitler's "Final Solution" scheme. The Russians were bursting with an overpowering revulsion. Our camp was one of many ignominious places that the Russian army had liberated. They brought calm to a devastative storm. The Russians, including the most hard-hearted soldiers, were overwhelmed by the evidential traces of horror. Our liberators deserved to be fêted with wine, wreaths of flowers, and embraced affectionately. However, we eerie shadows of human beings were astonished and overwhelmed with our serendipitous freedom, but we were far from being ecstatic. There was no round of huzzahs. The horror had indeed subsided but the calm had not entered my senses yet.

Starving and bedraggled, we did not show happy faces. We just could not. We were frozen in a crippling silence. We forgot how to talk, how to communicate, and how to smile. We were stone-faced, and you couldn't draw a tear or a smile from a stone. Our liberators were shocked facing our crinkled faces and slim figures, like stalks of celery, with dull expressionless looks and apathetic listlessness. We were cognizant that the victory over Nazism meant nothing to the dead in our families. We stood at the fences from inside the camp rather than outside the camp. It was as if we still belonged to that cursed prison. Paradoxically, the abhorrent and dangerous camp gave me a sense of shelter.

Holocaust survivors and their liberators marked the end of an unspeakable world war, and signified the beginning of a new life for those who endured. The act of liberation will always be seared in the minds and hearts of those inside and outside the gates of the camps. Jean Amery, a Holocaust Survivor, writes in one of her essays, "Anybody who was tortured will never again feel home in the world." Nevertheless, I looked at the Russian soldiers as my heroic liberators. We expected them to remove our mountains of despair. Still, I didn't feel triumphant. We all worried about our loved ones who had perished and would not be able to rejoice in our new freedom.

WANDERING AND WONDERING
HOW TO START A NEW LIFE

WHERE DO I GO?

The camp of deprivation and despair was horrible, but it was still a shelter! The only clothes I had were my inmate uniform. I pondered that if I should leave that place where would I get a piece of bread or a bed to sleep on? Where would I obtain my rudimentary needs? The US, British, and the French erected D.P. (displaced people) camps. In those camps, the ex-prisoners were sheltered, fed, clothed and assisted in many other ways. The Russians did not provide that. We were on our own. It felt like having a successful surgery, but the surgeon had walked away and left me on the operating table.

I had no idea how to get to my hometown to find out whether some other family members had survived. How should I pay for the transportation to go home, since I had no money? Would I ever have a place that I could call my home? Terrifying thoughts gnawed at my emaciated body and exhausted soul while gulping the elixir of liberty amid pell-mell circumstances. I wondered if I could ever go home again, because home would at best be a habitat mounted on ruins.

It was spring, and a time of newness and life. It was a wondrous time when plants were soaking in the warmth of the long-hidden sun. The beauty of nature blended with the rays of hope that the open gates of freedom might heal my physical and emotional wounds incurred by the Holocaust. Still, I was not exhilarated! I had a premonition that the future would be punctuated with hardship.

I was in poor health and had no strength to go to the city of Waldenburg. I continued to stay in the camp. I was languid and felt enslaved by the fear of the unknown. I slept on my bunk and ate whatever I could find in the camp's pantry.

GERMAN WOMEN

The German women who lived in the vicinity came to our camp on the day of liberation. They came because of fear that we might take vengeance and harm them. A middle-aged woman approached me. She put her hand on my shoulder and kissed my forehead. I had not felt a human touch for three years. The lady gave me a dish of cooked food and a shaggy beige sweater. When she noticed my piteous wounds, she sobbingly said, "We knew that there was a labor camp in this vicinity." She avoided using the dreaded name concentration camp. "We had no idea that you could have been so badly mistreated. I was blinded for so long, but now I can see the horror!" She muffled my inner cry! Then she said, "I just walked through several other rooms and heard some voices—some soft grunts. I turned around and I saw a living skeleton. Oh my God, it is so painful to see it. I am devastated and ashamed, I am so angry with Hitler. I have never liked him. I had to follow him because I feared him. How tragic it is that our husbands and children were pawns who were afraid not to obey Hitler's orders!" All the visiting Germans were outwardly sympathetic to us.

At that moment, the sirens of an ambulance reached my ears, and I wondered for whom they had come. I had not seen an ambulance or heard its siren during the years of my incarceration. This ambulance was called to help a German visitor to our camp who had fainted, apparently, shocked by confronting images of horror.

FRAU MERKEL

The following day, *Frau* (Mrs.) Merkel, brought sandwiches to me and to the other skeletons. When *Frau* Merkel wanted to know my first name, I told her "Alter." I pondered how sweet it was that I should no longer be nameless. Frau Merkel asked me if I would like to move temporarily into her house until I found something more suitable. I accepted her generous offer. I took my belongings, consisting of two pairs of shoes and two shirts (grabbed from the camp's storage room), the sweater she had given me, my camp bowl and spoon. I found the little and sparsely furnished room which I "rented" from *Frau* Merkel, to be an unexpected luxury.

She prepared a hot bathtub for me—a real indulgence. It was something I had been yearning for during years of my captivity. When I thanked her for the bath, she responded, "Our priest says you must help the needy and the oppressed. I am just doing that. Also, I had several Jewish friends before the war." She then invited me to take a seat on the porch to enjoy the sunshine. That day was so soothing to my scars! She served me a cup of milk with chocolate shavings. I felt so good, in fact too good. I said to *Frau* Merkel, "I feel that I have to apologize for being alive." She responded, "I try to understand the horror you went through, but please, you do not have to apologize. God wanted you to survive!" Then I asked her, "Would you know if there are any other Jews in Europe who have survived?" "I have no idea," she said embarrassingly.

There was a bed with a mattress, bed sheets, and pillows. After three years of having to sleep and eat on a bunk, my newfound luxuries afforded me a pleasurable night, albeit not a restful one, because of nightmares. It was the first time in my life that I had a room for myself. During my childhood, I shared a room with my brothers. We even shared the bed when we were little boys. Frau Merkel gave me clothing from her husband's wardrobe. He was a German MIA. I looked pathetic in those oversized clothes, but it felt good to have pockets again. I was very grateful for her support at the outset of my journey back to a new life. It was the first time in thirty-five months that when I opened my eyes in the morning, I saw no barbed wire and no guards. I did not have to line up for the head count or stand motionless in inclement weather. There was a little radio in the room. It gave me an opportunity to marvel at something that I had never before listened to.

The house was located in a small, quaint suburb, and I missed seeing other survivors. After several days, I ventured out to take a bus to the city of Waldenburg where many survivors gathered to catch up on the news and feasibility of venturing out and getting settled. Spring was in full bloom and the skies were clear. I paused to glance at the flower blossom. It was a renewal of life in all its majestic wonders.

HOSPITAL

On the way to the bus, I collapsed. All I remember is that I woke up in a hospital run by the Russian military. A Russian nurse, named Natashia, with a pretty face, was on duty in the section of a ward where I was lying. She cared for me beyond the norm and certainly in excess of her duty. She was affectionate and eventually introduced me to the passion of intimacy. She made all the amorous moves. Natashia fumigated my ravaged body of the lingering odor of decay. She took me out from a hellish aura and thrust me into a paradisiacal aroma. It was an enjoyable moment after years of having none. I pondered if I had committed a sin. On the other hand, I tried to convince myself that I had done nothing wrong. How could an embrace of mutual consent be sinful?

Because of the language barrier, I could not find out then what motivated Natashia, or what her true feelings were. There was no way to ask her why me—a homeless young Jewish boy, and five years her junior, tepid, and how a human husk had earned her love. My hands were thin and wiry while her hands were beautiful and sensual. Was it worthwhile for her to break military disciplinary rules? She was surrounded by many vigorous, experienced, steamy lovers and communicative men who could be more appealing than I could have ever been.

When my whiskers were irritating her face, Natashia asked a soldier to give me a shave and to show me how to shave. I had never shaved. I had no need to. Apparently, my hormones hindered to develop at the right time, because of the conditions in the camps.

Natasia, from Odessa in the Ukraine, was Jewish by birth. Her ID card identified her race as "Hebrew." (In communist Russia, Jews could not overtly practice their faith). It has often flitted across my mind that she was sympathetic to me as a Holocaust survivor. Natashia could not console me verbally because I did not understand Russian, so she had chosen to render comfort by smoothing my scars with her warm hands and personal charm. For me, she opened a gate of excitement. She provided me with an encounter that left me breathless and eager to experience it again. This extraordinary episode has been etched in my memory.

Soon after, Natashia's military unit moved away to another base, and I could never contact her again. This pleasant episode has indeed been a conundrum—a mystery for me ever since. Natasha introduced me to romance. I became a late bloomer with a roving eye.

PHOTOS

About five weeks after the liberation, I was still very feeble, homeless, and a pathetic mendicant. Nevertheless, the female survivor in the picture taken on June 10, 1945 was eight years my senior. I do not remember her name, but I do remember her passion. She knew when to turn the lights down and when to turn the heat up.

The other photos reflect the improved stages of my appearance. It is startling how three months of a relatively normal life can change a skeletal youngster into a healthy-looking man. The picture taken on August 15, 1945 in my prison garb is for me a souvenir and a constant reminder. Obviously, no inmate looked so robust in the camps.

6 / 10 / 1945

5 / 9 / 1945 - *Day of the Liberation*

6 / 15 / 1945

8 / 15 / 1945 - *With Pepka in Katowice*

8 / 15 / 1945

THE MILLER FAMILY

I was reluctant to go back to Mrs. Merkel because I wanted to stay in touch with other survivors who managed to find shelter in the city of Waldenburg. The city's social services department requested a German family in the city to give me shelter in their apartment. Mr. Miller was a clerk in the post office and Mrs. Miller was a homemaker. They had two daughters in their early twenties. The family was polite to me. Perhaps they were fearful that I might be seeking vengeance and would harm them. I felt that they did not like the municipality's imposition to set away a small room for me, and that they resented the mere presence of an "*untermench*" (a subhuman) residing in their midst. I sensed that in the body language of Mr. Miller. I also overheard some remarks the family made in the German language, which they had assumed that I did not understand, but I did.

Gertrud, one of the daughters, knocked at my door one evening and offered me a piece of cake. It was a nice gesture in times of scarcity. I graciously thanked her and anticipated that she would immediately exit my room. However, she asked me personal questions pertaining to the war, and the years of my affliction. I told her about the murder of my father, and my suspicion that all my relatives had perished. I spoke about the terrible conditions I was subjected to in the camps. She commiserated and wept. "You are breaking my heart," she said." The Nazis broke my life and probably God's heart," I said. She responded to this by saying, "How will I ever be able to explain to my children the abominable behavior of my generation under Hitler?" Gertrud continued, "I once had a horrible dream that Hitler would lose the war and bring misery to all Germans. When I told my father about my dream, he told me to consult a psychiatrist."

At that point, she nudged me, took a chair, and sat next to me. While lingering on she put her hand on my lap, kissed my hand, and hugged me very affectionately. I was besotted. Her nubile body stirred my loins and I trembled but was not sure how to respond. My natural impulses and my belated stirrings of manhood were suppressed by emotions. She was young and pretty but she was a German woman. How could I possibly become intimate with a member of a society that had vowed to annihilate my family? My lust evaporated instantly. Gertrud was not like Natashia. The Russian nurse and I were both victims of the German genocidal policies. When we eventually returned to our hometowns, we both found our ancestral homes destroyed! I did not, and perhaps could not make any amorous advances. Gertrude left my room seemingly disappointed.

Waldenburg was part of the area that had been annexed to Poland (as agreed upon by the Allies). In July, about two months after the liberation, things started to stabilize. Some survivors settled, temporarily, within the city and the suburbs of Waldenburg. There was a soup kitchen run by German and Holocaust survivors. I received some clothing and a few marks from the social service department in Waldenburg. Most survivors tried to reach their hometowns in order to find out what had happened to their families, and to check the possibilities of starting a new life on blood-soaked grounds, in the towns and villages in which they had lived before the war.

MR. SCHMIDT

One day, while strolling in the streets of Waldenburg, I spotted Mr. Schmidt, one of the guards in the Waldenburg concentration camp. He obviously was not wearing his military uniform and had grown a mustache. I said to him, *"Gut morgen Herr Schmid,* (Good morning Mr. Schmidt). He did not recognize me, or perhaps he did not want to recognize me for fear that I might report him to the Russians. Frankly, I had no intention to do so. My frame of mind was not for revenge. No matter how I was hurting, I let it go and did not try to get even. He said to me, "I was sorry then to see how you were mistreated in that Waldenburg camp. Please believe me that I did not ask to become a guard in a concentration camp; I was forced to. It was a very banal job. I personally just followed orders. You have to understand that as a German soldier I had to carry out disdainful duties. I was disgusted with banality of evil, but I had to disregard the impulses of my heart. Is there anything I could help you with now?" I responded, "No thank you, but I would appreciate it if you could spare some change, so I could buy some bread." He gave me a ten deutsche mark. I thanked him and I felt rich.

When he realized that I would not harm him, he continued to talk to me. "I am one of the few guards who chose to stay in this area. Most guards fled towards the American zone. They felt that the Americans and the British would be more benevolent than the vengeful Russians would. I stayed here because of my family. We had a small house in a suburb of Waldeburg. The house was bombarded and destroyed. My wife and three children are missing. I still hope that they have somehow survived. I have been searching and inquiring everywhere. We all paid a high price for Hitler's aggression. I live now in a small trailer parked in the park not far from the camp that you were in. Come to see me sometime." Mr. Smith slithered away like an eel.

This encounter reminded me of the biblical story when Joseph's brothers didn't recognize him when they came to Egypt to buy provisions for their families due to the famine in the land of Canaan. Thirteen years earlier the brothers had sold Joseph into slavery because they hated him for being Jacob's favorite son. Joseph, who successfully deciphered Pharaoh's dreams, was appointed by Pharaoh to be in charge of the food supply in Egypt. Joseph said to his brothers, "Do you know who I am? I am your brother Joseph, the one you tried to kill by throwing him into a pit and then sold him into slavery." Joseph could have avenged himself, but he had chosen not to do so. "Do not be afraid; I shall not harm you. I shall give you all the food you need," Joseph said.

Had I handed Mr. Smith over to the Russians, they might have killed him, and I would have felt bad. God says in Ezekiel 33, "I have no pleasure in the death of the wicked."

GROSS-MASSELWITZ

I took the train to look for the noble German woman who had risked her life by hiding sandwiches for me.

I inquired everywhere, including the city hall. People looked at me and wondered if I was sane. How can you have a river without water? How can you locate somebody if you do not know the person's name and address? All I could say, or rather pray, was, "May God reward her."

BACK TO POLAND—TO CHRZANÓW

I took my few personal belongings and said good-bye to the Miller family where I had sojourned for a few weeks. I boarded a train for a free ride, because I did not have money to pay the fare. Most of the repatriates were penniless. The train was very crowded with Czechs, Jews, Poles, Russians, and others. All of us were bedeviled, confused, and absorbed in worrisome thoughts in anticipation of reaching our destinations. It was a very arduous trip. The train chugged through the German and Polish cities and countryside, which was disgraced by vast areas of pulverized buildings in industrial and residential areas. There were charred and mangled vehicles everywhere. A putrid mess of a devastative war spoiled the beautiful scenery. Our train stalled frequently. Jaded and hungry, I finally reached Chrzanów.

IN CHRZANÓW

I walked from the railroad station to 12 Pierackiego Street, my home where I had been living from childbirth until the day of deportation. As I walked, I felt squashing memories. I frequently looked behind me, wondering who was going to beat me. I had developed the habit during my three years in captivity.

The staircase leading to my apartment witnessed my joy mixed with anxiety. I knocked at the front door and told the Polish occupant that I had survived the war, and would like to look at my former home. The man slammed the door in my face. I was dumbfounded and very distraught. I did not know where to turn. I was a migrant seeking shelter—a place to stay and I could not find one.

Emotionally and physically exhausted, I went to the Jewish cemetery. It was a familiar path on hallowed grounds. I paid a visit to my mother's grave and then to my father's mass grave. While there, I recited a short prayer. Night fell and I spent the night on the grave. I was soaked with rage and grief. I prayed, "Please God, do not turn your face from me." Although I was a frequent visitor to the cemetery, I dreaded the ghostly stillness. I felt that the entire city of Chrzanów was one big graveyard. This cemetery was just several miles away from the largest Jewish cemetery in the world—Auschwitz—a cemetery without even one headstone.

On my way back, I noticed a little house where the patio was paved with tombstones from the Jewish cemetery. It was a painful and shameful sight.

I was dismayed by the notion that my apartment was occupied by a malevolent Pole who probably slept with his wife in my parents' bed. I wondered whether social justice would take hold with the liberation from Nazi bondage. My procrastinated homelessness was very distressful. I was eager to water my roots, yet there was no helping hand in sight. Most Poles seemed to be ostracizing me. I felt as if I was pulling a sled with no snow on the ground. I fretted that one bad move might have fateful consequences. There was still so much hurt in my heart, and I felt defeated. The following day I went morosely back to my former home and knocked at the door of every neighbor in that building which had twenty-four apartments.

All of the tenants were Poles who took over the vacated apartments of the Jewish deported tenants. Few pre-war tenants recognized me; some were happy to see me alive. One young Polish neighbor told me, "You look so gaunt but your piercing and sparkling eyes are the same." It lifted me up! Some made snide remarks. Others said nothing and they stared at me as if I were a leper or radioactive. One tenant welcomed my survival and gave me good tidings, saying "Come in and meet your two cousins." I was overwhelmed with joy that Mania and Berish (Ben) Wiener had survived. This brought the number of known survivors of our extended family to three. Mania and Ben came back to their apartment and the current occupant let them stay in one of the rooms until they could find another accommodation. My cousins were luckier than I was when the present occupant of my apartment did not even let me peek in. My heart ached, but there was nothing I could have done in that chaotic post-war situation. The nascent municipal officials were not helpful to me. I felt powerless, as though I was just withering away. Recurring difficulties told me that my battle for survival was not over. My stomach was in knots as I pondered where to turn. My march towards normalcy was far away. A shack with a bed and a table would have satisfied me. A place at somebody else's table could have alleviated my hunger and loneliness. The alien universe was reluctant to take me back into its folds. I heard that some Holocaust survivors who encountered hostility from the Poles had killed themselves in desperation.

Three sisters of the Singer family, our pre-war neighbor, survived and found shelter in an empty one-room apartment in our building. They welcomed me effusively. Noticing that I was scruffy and penniless, the sisters offered me to stay with them. I graciously accepted their willingness to share their scanty dwellings with me, a nineteen-year-old adolescent male. Pepka, twelve years my senior, and one of the three sisters who knew my biological mother, had always related to me affectionately.

The sisters borrowed a sewing machine and started making dresses, which was their vocation in pre-war years. They shared with me whatever they could buy with their meager income. Pepka was very gracious and warm. She often complimented me on my good looks, which resembled my mother's features.

I had not taken off my shabby clothes since arriving in Chrzanów. I had not taken a shower for a long time because I could not find one. In the Singer's apartment there was no shower room. Pepka warmed some water on the stove and improvised a washing corner. She purchased new underwear, shirts, and a tie and jacket for me. She laundered everything that I had worn for the last few weeks. Above, there is a photo of the two of us.

I went to see the *Beth-Midrash*, the synagogue that my father belonged to and where I had attended services during my early childhood. The synagogue was sometimes so crowded that there wasn't even standing room. Now, I found the synagogue crumbling. It was being used as a storage house. I felt desolated!

Although I walked unshackled, painful memories enveloped me wherever I went in Chrzanów, the little hometown that I knew so well. Each building, each house of worship, and each street and alley wailed with me. I wept, and my tears drenched the grounds that had been soaked with the blood of people I was so close to. I roamed the streets through memory lanes. Looking at the facades of familiar buildings, I was eager to see a familiar face. I was hungry for food and for a casual greeting. Plodding through the streets, I tried to retrace pleasant memories from my early childhood, pondering, "I have cried out with tears, and now it is time for a new start." I toyed with the idea of restructuring a new life in Chrzanów. When a tornado knocks down a tree but leaves a surviving twig, we can plant it and eventually the new tree will bear fruits with the same flavor that the original tree had.

Many Poles who noticed me turned their heads. Some of them threw hostile glances at me. My emaciated body, my lethargic walk, and my disheveled and shabby clothes revealed my identity. I was a Jew, a Holocaust survivor, and I was an unwelcome returnee. Some Poles who

75

took over or stole Jewish properties fretted at the possibility of having to return their loot to the legitimate owners. I could not find, neither could I afford a decent lodging. I was gawked at but not pitied. The few survivors who were remnants of a deeply rooted Jewish community, ten thousand strong, were not welcomed back. Deep-seated anti-Semitism could not countenance the survival of a Jewish community remnant. This phenomenon just added to the indignities beset upon me during the war years. Eventually, only a very few survivors resettled in Chrzanów, and those few who had, by now, have passed away. **There is not a single Jew living in Chrzanów today**.

The survivors had no stamina and received no support at that time from any quarter to rebuild their life in their birthright's environment. News about pogroms and the slaughter of forty-six returning survivors in Kielce and three in Przytyk, and the riots against Jews in Kraków was utterly heartbreaking. Although anti-Semitism was not obligatory (it was not the official government policy), old anti-Semites were invigorated because the local police did little to stop the slaughter, and sometimes were even complicit. There were reports from other cities in Poland stating that Jewish survivors were slain. New fear and mental perturbation enveloped my existence. There was a renascent anti-Semitism. It reminded me of the small Polish town of Jedwabne where 1,600 Jewish residents were murdered by native Poles in a single day during July 1941. It is a shame that many Poles hated the Jews, despite the remarkable contribution of the Jewish people in all aspects of society. A wave of gloom came over me. I was yearning to return to my cherished roots, but the blood-drenched soil of Poland apparently was thirsty for more Jewish blood. Traditional Polish inimical sentiments had been invigorated by the Nazis cultivation of anti-Semitism. As the days fled by, a secure life seemed increasingly elusive. I was like a nomad in the desert looking for green pastures, but could not find any. Neither could I find a path through the maze of the unknown. Displaced and disoriented, I decided to leave Chrzanów and perhaps Poland.

My cousin Mania knew that our parents had buried some jewelry in the cellar where the coal was stored. Not remembering the exact location, we stealthily began digging with primitive tools for many long hours. We finally did find several gold chains and necklaces. Mania, Ben, and I shared equally the uncovered throve. For me, this serendipitous find, in exchange for currency, sustained me for a while. It also made me feel good that the Nazis had not found it. It would have helped their war-machine.

IN KRAKÓW

From the proceeds I obtained from selling the unearthed jewelry, I bought food and other basic necessities. I paid my train fare to Krakow. I was no longer begging for money but I was still unable to afford shelter or buy enough food.

In Krakow, I roamed the streets and met survivors who told me that the American Jewish Distribution Committee (JOINT) was providing survivors with temporary shelter in a rented community hall. When I reached that hall, I was delighted to find my cousin, Frania (Frances) Wiener. That unexpected rendezvous made me realize that four cousins of our extended family had survived the Holocaust

No Jewish agency, not even the Red Cross, was able at that time, to provide reliable information about who had survived the war. If their records indicated that a certain individual did survive, his or her current address was not available.

I was in a Kraków hospital at the age of six when I broke my leg. I remembered nothing about the city from that time. In school, I learned about the historical, legendary, and beautiful big city of Kraków. Now, I heard about the sorrows and tragedies that beset Kraków under the German occupation. Most of the 70,000 Jews lived in the Jewish Quarter of the Kazimietz district. They had perished in the Nazi death camps, forced labor camps, and the most notorious was Plaszów. Auschwitz and Birkenau were only forty miles west of Kraków.

Jewish literature bubbles over with stories from Krakow—the fabled *golem* (boor), the wisdom of the rabbis, the matchmaking, the market days, and communal life. Only 2,000 local Jews survived the Holocaust. A further anti-Semitic government campaign in 1968 forced many to leave. Today, there are about 200 Jews living in Krakow. Most of them are elderly Holocaust survivors.

As a man in hard straits without a home and no money, I was rolling the dice. I did not have a clue where to turn for help. Still, I rejoiced in every minute of my freedom. I spent my days ambling along the avenues of Krakow. The Poles loved that city so dearly that they declared the city an open city, and the Germans conquered it without a fight. I reached the Market Square which has long been the cultural and intellectual center of Poland. The Square is 656 yards long and 656 yards wide. It is reportedly the largest such public space in Europe. I was impressed by the architecture of the old St. Mary's Church with its gold-flecked spires.

Despite all the difficulties I encountered trying to re-establish myself, my freedom and my improved health were reflected in my looks. My exuberance for life surged. Sitting ruminatively on a bench in the Square, a Polish lady, Maria, in her thirties, initiated a conversation with me. She listened diligently and sympathetically to my war tribulations and realized how much better off she had been, in comparison to me under the German occupation. After a while, she tapped my shoulder, wished me good luck, and sauntered away. She turned the corner and was out of my sight.

The following day, I took a stroll, eager to make contact with any willing stranger. I was beset with a teenager's longings—soul-searching and self-doubt. I was trying to find an answer to my tormenting questions. I was basking in the liberty I had recently gained and wondered if I would be granted the right to shape my life.

I paused at the bench I had occupied the previous day. While ruminating of painless days, pleasurable moments, and fantasizing about that woman from the day before, she unexpectedly appeared and asked me, "Are you in a reverie?"

I was pleasantly surprised to see her again. My body trembled with excitement. "Yes, indeed," I said.

She was charming and had a lively air and amiable disposition. A tiny gold crucifix on a silver chain hung from her neck. I realized that she was a Christian, probably a Catholic, as most Poles were. For a while I felt apprehensive. She had put me at ease when she had expressed her feelings and views about the war. She gave me a sign of acceptance and a welcome antidote to the unwelcome gestures shown by some Poles. She told me that before the war, she had had many Jewish neighbors. We chatted for about two hours. When I told her that I was reluctantly going back to the community hall where one has no privacy, she surprisingly offered me to sleep at her house.

"You might be more comfortable there," she said.

I accepted her gracious offer with bated breath. She slipped her arm into mine and we walked, appearing to others, as mother and son. I was wondering whether that fortuitous encounter portended a ticket out of my predicament. Her small apartment was furnished in good taste. She had a large mirror in a flowery bedroom. The monogrammed pillows reminded me of the pillows I had slept on in my parents' home, and so did the embroidered cushions on the sofa in the living room. Her modest apartment was in my eyes a mansion that I had not seen for many years.

I was wondering what was in store for me in that pleasant environment. It really perked me up. I was grateful for her kindness and enjoyed a convivial and delicious supper. The nutritious meal energized my body and lifted my spirit. She had China dishes and long-necked-glass jugs. The bowl of colorful fruits dazzled me, and I was drunk from the aroma permeating the room. She tried to whet my appetite and gave me a tremendous amount of affection. It was a refreshing moment for me since my amorous days with Natashia.

Maria confidentially told me that her husband, while serving in the Polish army, was wounded and had become impotent. She shunned chastity and engaged in an adulterous affair. Her husband, Janek, divorced her when he had found out about her affair. Our social evening evolved into an amorous night where I was probably expected to be sexually prowess. I steeled myself to be, but regretfully, my emaciated body was not apt to it yet. Still, Maria's engulfing passion exhilarated both of us. The following morning Maria went to work and I had to go back to the Jewish shelter. I felt jilted by Maria. The frolicsome fling with sexual Maria made me aware of my impotency. However, with the passing of several months, my body rejuvenated.

I roamed the streets of Krakow trying to make contact with other survivors hoping that they might know where to turn for help. I had been a liberated person for four months but I was still in a dazed condition. Beset by health problems, anxiety, and loneliness, I was desperate and wanted to put an end to my languishing. I wanted to find a place to sleep on a full stomach. I always carried everything with me that I possessed. I was never sure where I would find a peaceful corner of privacy.

I learned from another survivor that a Jewish agency in Sosnowiec was organizing groups of homeless survivors to go to Palestine. I liked the idea of going to Palestine because I knew that two uncles and two aunts (my mother's siblings) had left Poland in the early 1930s to escape poverty and oppression. As pioneers to that arid land, they toiled the soil of our ancestors. I left Kraków for Katowice by train. Soon thereafter, I went to Sosnowiec, where I joined a small group of fifty survivors—camp internees, partisan fighters, and Jews emerging from their hiding places. Several emissaries from The Jewish Agency in Palestine arrived in Poland to assist the remnants (about 400,000) of the once flourishing Jewish population of 3.5 million.

A DISPLACED PERSON
IN CZECHOSLOVAKIA,
AUSTRIA, AND ITALY

IN CZECHOSLOVAKIA

We lingered for several weeks in shabby places in Sonowiec. In September 1945, we were led to a rendezvous point at the Polish-Czechoslovakian border.

A "contact man" smuggled us into Czechoslovakia. This was a starting point of an arduous and long journey to the promised land of Palestine. For several days, we stayed in a dingy hotel in Prague where we lacked comfort and adequate food. On *Yom Kippur*, I prayed in the main synagogue, which had just been reopened by Czechoslovakian Jews who were also Holocaust survivors (315,000 Czech Jews perished in the Holocaust—88 percent of its prewar community).

This was the first High Holy Day that I could observe since the liberation. All the pews in the synagogue were occupied and I could only find standing room. It was refreshing to see so many congregated surviving Jews. An usher handed me a *Machzor*, (prayers for the holy day) I could pray from a book rather than reciting prayers from memory, as I had to do in the camps. The services concluded at sunset.

A lady in her 40s glanced at me with moistened eyes and asked me something in Czechoslovakian which I did not understand. She

81

switched to a halting Yiddish that enabled us somehow to converse. She asked me to join her in breaking the fast. After walking several blocks with her, we reached her apartment. The sign on the door read, "Rachel Spiegel." The sparsely furnished apartment was indicative of a new beginning and of a life renewed. Rachel told me that her husband had perished in the Holocaust, and that her older son did not come back from the army. Her younger son had apparently perished in a concentration camp.

Then she said, "I miss my family and feel uncomfortable to be the only survivor of my immediate family. I am only aware of one niece who survived, and she is on her way to Palestine."

Suddenly Rachel broke down. Sobbingly she said, "You look like my younger son, Shmuel, and I could not stop staring from the moment I noticed you at the entrance of the synagogue.

She embraced me and I sobbingly said, "My older brother, Shmuel, with the same name as your son, apparently perished, and my stepmother's name was Rachel the same as yours."

What a coincidence! After a three-hour stay in her house, I had to go back to my group's temporary shelter. Rachel asked me to come to the synagogue on the next Sabbath and then come for dinner after the services. One day later, our group was moved to a D.P. (Displaced People) camp. There were no telephones, and I had no way of contacting her to say good-bye. Inadvertently, I forgot to jot down her address and thus regretfully lost contact with Rachel forever.

I remember visiting the Old Jewish Cemetery, where many famous rabbis are buried including the *Maharal* of Prague, Rabbi Yehuda Leow (1510-1609) who was a revered Talmudic scholar and author of books in philosophy and ethics. Rabbi Shneur Zalman, founder of the *Chabad* movement was a great-grandson of the *Maharal*.

From Prague, we were driven to Bratislava, and after a short stay, we were driven to the Czech-Austrian border.

IN AUSTRIA

Again, a "contact man" smuggled us into Austria where we were accommodated in a Vienna dingy hotel. After several days, we were moved to a D.P. camp in Trofojach, near Graz. It was operated by British personnel who liberated that part of Austria. We joined hundreds of other Jewish refugees who had already been in that camp.

There were no dining halls or any other facilities where we could sit down. We had to eat on our beds in the barracks. It was not comfortable but it was a luxury in comparison to what we had five months earlier while still being in Nazis hands.

One day, standing in line towards the kitchen counter, Deborah, who ladled the soup, said to me, "This is probably not enough for you. Come later and I shall give you another portion."

I did go, and Deborah had a container ready for me. I thanked her for her help. To my question where she was from, she said, "Come to barrack 9, about 7:00 p.m., and I shall tell you my life story."

I went to her barrack and asked her, "Was I the only one in the line who you offered a second portion?"

"Well, I wish I could do the same for many others, but we are not in a position to do so. I just had a big lunch and felt like skipping supper. I wanted to give you my allotted portion."

I asked, "Why me?"

"You resemble my brother who perished in Auschwitz."

Deborah introduced me to ten women who shared the same compartment of a long barrack that held about 100 Holocaust female survivors.

We conversed in Yiddish. Deborah also spoke fluent Hungarian and Czechoslovakian. She was born in Ruthenia, known as the Carpathian Ukraine region of Czechoslovakia. In 1939, when Bohemia and Moravia became "a Protectorate" of Germany, Ruthenia was awarded to Hungary. In 1941, Hungary joined the Axis. The Germans persecuted the Jews there like in the other conquered lands of Europe. Eventually, Deborah and her parent were sent to Auschwitz. Deborah survived but her entire family perished. She told me," *A haboru alatt mindent elveszitettem ami nekem kedves es ertekes volt"* (During the war I lost everything that was dear to me!).

Deborah and I had a similar religious upbringing. However, after the war Deborah adhered to the practice of Jewish orthodoxy and I did not. I still believed in the divine but I was angry with God and became less religiously observant. Those differences did not interfere with our romantic relationship. Still, I respected her beliefs.

She once told me, "Out of deep respect and love for my departed parents, who were very pious, it became incumbent upon me to continue the tradition that they had practiced."

I accepted her explanation. Most Holocaust survivors were inclined to liberate themselves from some religious restraints.

Deborah told me, in the Hungarian language, *"Most viszont a kedvessegednek vagyok a rabja; vagyom a szereteted utan. Elviselhetetlen lenne szamomra, ha elveszitenelek"* (I am a victim of your charm. I am starving for your love. It would be unbearable for me to lose you.). Deborah repeatedly expressed her desire to marry me and have a large family—to convince the Nazis that their aim to annihilate the Jewish people had failed.

Deborah was a sweetheart. She loved to read, knit, cook, and she celebrated life. I shall never forget how she used her infinitesimal allowance to buy wool to knit a sweater for me. It was beautiful and so was her fetching voice. She had an unflagging interest in music. Deborah put on her emotional clothes and sang soulful songs by the light of the full moon. Her songs of love, nature, and faith were in three different languages. She would not miss one evening of singing paeans for me.

She told me, "My heart is bursting with song that sprouts from my soul." It was reminiscent of the song of the Biblical Deborah (Judges 5).

We laughed through tears when we talked about our childhoods. We cried in each other's arms when we talked about our parents and our families. She said, "Without my family, I am like a hibiscus plant that has shed its pink leaves. Share your heart with me. The only consolation for me would be if you marry me and we had a large family. This would please our dear parents in their resting places."

In December 1945, the group I belonged to was awakened in the early morning hours. We had twenty minutes to stealthily board trucks, which were parked outside the camp. We were not told where the next stop would be on the route to our anticipated destination of Palestine. I woke Deborah to say good-bye. We embraced and promised to trace each other's locations upon our arrival in Palestine.

We alighted from the trucks in Willach, near the Austrian-Italian border, at a D.P. camp run by the Austrians. There was no way I could have made contact with Deborah. There were no telephones, and my mail was returned with "Addressee Unknown."

The harsh winter aggravated my arthritic condition to such an extent that I could not move. An Austrian doctor suggested surgery on my spine to relieve my excruciating back pains. It was a thin strand on which to hang my hopes for a healthier body. Having no relative to consult, I had to trust my instinct. I decided against the operation. Had I submitted myself to that surgeon's advice, I could have been crippled for life. After three weeks of living in those difficult surroundings, they moved us to the Italian border.

IN ITALY

In January 1946, soldiers of the Palestine Hebrew Brigades—Palestinian Jews who volunteered to serve in the British forces as distinguished fighting units—drove us in covered trucks to Italy. It was a long drive before we arrived at Mestera, near Venice. The weather was warmer than in Austria, and I joined a group of ten comrades for a trip to Venice. We enjoyed the beauty of the city, although we had no money to buy anything that our eyes desired. Growing up in a little town in Poland, I had never seen floodgates or such beautiful scenery. After several days, we were moved to Madjento, a small town near Milan.

We were sheltered in an abandoned house which had been taken over by the British Army. The Palestine Hebrew Brigade provided us with our necessities and services such as medical care. At that juncture, I was still in poor health. My digestive system was unable to absorb all kinds of food. I was quite lethargic and could not participate in many physical activities that the brigade soldiers initiated to rejuvenate the Holocaust survivors. A great "treat" was a trip to Milan to tour the city, and in the evening to see a show at the *La Scala*, the renowned opera house. For me, it was the first time in my life that I had watched an opera or any other theatrical play.

Italian women in the neighborhood of our base were very friendly. I did not speak Italian, but body language worked well.

A twenty-year-old Ukrainian girl in our group, Rivkale, and I became very friendly. She was short, stout, and had radiant brown eyes that grew brighter when we spent time together. She congratulated me on my nineteenth birthday. It was the first time in my life that somebody marked the day. As a child, birthdays in my culture were not celebrated with cakes or greeting cards. Rivkale grew up in a poor family with ten siblings. The Nazis dragged her immediate family into a synagogue and set the entire structure on fire with all the Jewish captives inside.

Rivkale eluded the Germans by escaping to a nearby forest. Later, she joined the Jewish partisans. We conversed in Yiddish. We chatted about our communities' lore and swapped our tragic war experiences. I was astonished and saddened to hear her talk about the terrible conditions that prevailed in the forests. There was a lack of food and shelter. There was always fear of being discovered by the Germans, and there was an added danger of attacks by beasts of prey. Rivkale strove to survive because she loved life, and she knew how to enjoy the little pleasures that life had to offer. She wished to survive as a remnant of her family. Despite her traumatic past, Rivkale was full of life and hope.

Several weeks prior to the burning of the synagogue, her uncle and his entire family were rounded up and taken to a killing field to dig their own graves. They were ordered to take off their clothes, and then they were shot. Not all shots killed the victims instantly. Many were buried alive. Rivkale wept while describing to me that tragic event. Apparently, it was too far to bring Jews from the Ukraine to the death camps in Poland, so they were liquidated locally. Hundreds of thousands of Russian Jews were murdered by the *Einsatzgrupen* (special mobile units) by the end of 1941. When the Nazis were planning to invade the U.S.S.R., they decided at the same time to annihilate its Jewish population.

Rivkale had a kind word to say about everybody except the ones who were lazybones and who had puffy egos.

Despite so much suffering, there was no room in Rivkale's heart for hatred or prejudice. There was a fine analytical mind with a rich imagination behind Rivkale's trite façade. Rivkale had come from a secular family, and had a circle of liberal friends. Her big brain, her warm heart, her common sense, and her friendly banter lifted my spirit.

After two weeks in Madjento, we were driven to the coastal city of Genoa where 250 refugees were lodged for several weeks in an abandoned mansion—reportedly owned by an Italian fascist. It was quite crowded, but we were happy to hear from the emissaries that our refugee status would soon terminate by settling in Palestine. I just wondered how many more hills and valleys I would have to traverse en

Rivkale and me in Tradate, Italy - **4 / 14 / 1946**

route to our final destination. I was eager to leave my victim-baggage and my refugee status behind me. I wanted to have a chance to find work, and perhaps to acquire a skill. Termination of my dependency on institutional and charitable room and board would be refreshing. I desired to assume responsibility and gain control on my life.

Soldiers from the Palestine Hebrew Brigade visited us, used their free time to teach us the rudiments of the Hebrew language, and introduced us to the history of our ancestral land. They briefed us about the achievements of contemporary Jewish settlers in Palestine and taught us other elementary subjects. I was very appreciative of the soldiers who had devoted their free time to us. Their sympathy and spirit rekindled my hope. I shall never forget one soldier, Asher Mittleman, a fatherly figure who became a prop for me, and an inspiration to us all. That opportunity to learn was an impetus to a new life—a breathless surge of hope.

For some unexplained reason, (end of February 1946) we were transferred to Tradatte where we stayed in a *Castello*an (an old castle) that housed about 800 refugees. Here, too, we got support from the Palestine Hebrew Brigade, as well as from other Jewish emissaries from Palestine. By the end of May 1946, we were ordered to destroy any personal documents and anything that might reveal our refugee status. We were not told why.

We boarded trucks with the insignia of the Palestine Hebrew Brigade, which brought us to an undisclosed shore in Italy. The emissaries from the Jewish Agency told us that we would be sailing *Aliyah Bet* (illegally). The British authorities did not sanction us to sail to Palestine. In order to appease the Arabs living in Palestine under the British Mandate, the British government had issued the "White Paper" in 1939 which limited Jewish immigration to 1,500 a month. The aggregate total was not to exceed 75,000 by the year 1944. Thus, the historical Balfour Declaration (1917) was being warped by politics.

At sundown, the skies foreboded a storm. Thirteen hundred of us boarded a decrepit ship—the Josiah Wedgwood. Our hopes for a better future were marred by the poor conditions on the ship. It was very crowded. We had no hot meals, just crackers and cheese. Even our water was rationed. Many of the passengers got seasick. That merchant ship was converted into a transport vehicle for Holocaust survivors.

There was no ventilation and the sanitary facilities were very primitive. The atmosphere was quite tense. A mixture of families with small children (born to partisans in the forests of Europe) and many young adults of diverse political affiliations sometimes caused heated debates and friction. I felt drained. Despite all the discomfort and disharmony among the passengers, there was the hope and expectation of reaching the Holy Land.

As we approached the port of Haifa, the captain of the ship told us, **"If the British catch our ship and expel us from the shores of Palestine, I will sink the ship with all the people on it."**

Surprisingly, there was no outcry or voices of opposition from the exhausted refugees.

ARRIVING AT THE FINAL DESTINATION

THE LANDING IN PALESTINE

We had been at sea for ten days when we were surrounded by three British war ships that escorted us to the Palestinian port of Haifa. When our ship tried to evade the British blockade, the marines fired above our heads as a warning. My stomach twisted and churned; it was a terrible trauma for all of us. We were gritting our teeth and clinging grimly to the battered hope for a peaceful landing.

Upon arrival at Haifa, the British soldiers boarded our ship and again fired warning shots into the air. We were told that all of us would be sent to a detention camp because we came illegally to Palestine. This was very exasperating. Once again, I was put behind a barbed wire in Athlit, outside the city of Haifa. The British constructed this large internment camp for the refugees—Holocaust survivors who tried to reach the shores of Palestine by *Aliya Bet*. Athlit—the British named it a "clearance" camp—was guarded by the British police and operated by the Jewish Agency of Palestine. I was interned for ten days in that dank place and released on July 7, 1946 (as reflected in the note below).

KIBBUTZ

Prior to the release from Athlit, officials from the Jewish Agency of Palestine came to interview us. Most of the refugees had pre-arranged

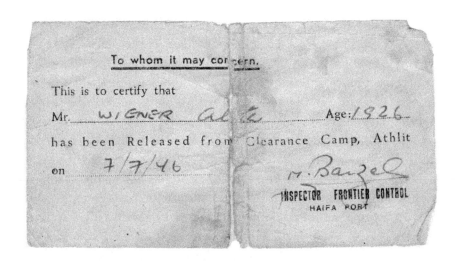

To whom it may concern,

This is to certify that

Mr. WIGNER Albert .... Age: 1926

has been Released from Clearance Camp, Athlit

on 7/7/46

M. Barzel

INSPECTOR FRONTIER CONTROL
HAIFA PORT

locations where they could go to live with relatives and friends. I did not know the addresses of my uncles and aunts. I could hardly remember their first names and I had no idea if they were alive.

Since I was not in a position to direct the officials where I would like to go to, they sent me away with several other lonely souls to a "kibbutz"—a collective farm in Gan-Schmuel, near Chedera.

On arrival, I was put up in a tent with three other new arrivals. Each occupant was furnished with an empty (fruit) box in which to keep our personal belongings. It was a year since the liberation. I had been wandering since then, but now I had my semi-private corner in a friendly environment. In the evening, the secretary of the kibbutz officially welcomed us.

The next morning, following breakfast in the communal dining room, I was assigned to pick oranges. It was hard work and I spent long hours under the scorching sun. I was exhausted from hard labor and the nights were sleepless due to the heat and the biting mosquitoes. Nevertheless, I was content with my new surroundings. It was a welcome respite to be on friendly grounds. There were no Nazi brutes to harass and beat me. The *Chaverim* (members/friends) of the commune were very sympathetic to us Holocaust survivors. Most of the kibbutz members had lost relatives in the Holocaust. Some members tried to alleviate the psychological, bureaucratic, and cultural issues with new immigrants, especially refugees, who had to cope within a new underdeveloped country. At meal times, sitting at various tables in the communal dining hall, we eventually got acquainted with all members of the kibbutz. Since I did not know modern/spoken Hebrew, I could communicate only with those who still remembered Yiddish.

I found most of the members of the kibbutz to be hard working, honest, idealistic, and cordial. It seemed to me as an evolving utopian society. Members received no salaries, and everybody contributed to the welfare of the commune according to his or her ability. The commune provided everyone with all the basic necessities.

We spent most of our free evenings studying the Hebrew language or listening to guest speakers. At times, we attended a stage performance put on by members of the kibbutz, or an outside group of professional entertainers.

During and after the Holocaust, the *Yishuv* (Jewish community in Palestine) and the world Jewry had been urging the British Mandate to revoke the "White Paper." There was an urgent need to resettle hundreds of thousands of displaced people, mainly Holocaust survivors, who still lingered in D.P. camps in Germany. There was a political and an armed struggle going on at the same time when I arrived in Palestine. The *Yishuv* also had to defend itself against the Arabs who had been vigorously rejecting the Zionist aspirations of reclaiming their ancient land. Many Jews joined the *Hagana* (Jewish underground defense force) to be trained for fighting the Arab attackers and resist the British soldiers who forbade the establishment of Jewish defense units. Becoming part of the kibbutz, I was expected to join the ranks of the *Hagana*. I was girded for a kind of battle that I could not have anticipated to evolve in my lifetime.

TEL-AVIV

Three weeks after settling in the kibbutz, I had two days off and went with several other *olim* (newcomers) to see the Jewish metropolis of *Eretz-Israel* (Land of Israel).

Seeing Jews walking freely, I wondered if it was for real. The people seemed to be so normal. I wondered if I was fit to live among them. Was I normal? Would I ever be normal? What is the purpose of my life? Why had I survived, one out of so many? What was my duty?

Whatever I saw bewildered me. Men and women were joyful. The beaches were full of sunbathers, and there was not one emaciated body among them. It seemed to me a hedonistic epicenter in a land of austerity. Alenby Street was awash with ritzy shops and boutiques. I had no money to buy anything but at least I could window shop, which was something I had never done before. There were no Nazis around to beat me, and if there were other enemies, we now had the means to beat them back. A Jewish police officer passed by and said hello to me, and I did not have to take off my cap and bow my head. In fact, I felt like taking off my hat as a gesture of admiration in contrast to the days when I had to do that as an act of humiliation. Was I in a wonderland? The people bartered staples I had never seen. The city was a bustle. It was a fascinating window into a normal life.

I put on a bathing suit that I had borrowed from the kibbutz and sat on the beach watching happy children playing, pretty girls parading, and amateurs entertaining. What a different world from the one I had endured just one year earlier. Near me, there was a middle-aged couple sitting on beach chairs under an umbrella. I was sitting on the sand because I had no money to rent a beach chair.

The couple noticed a scar on my leg and the lady approached me. She said, "I am sorry to see such a young man with scars. What happened to you? Were you hurt by an Arab?"

"No," I said. "I am a Holocaust survivor. This scar is just one of the many physical and mental scars from Nazi Germany!"

She responded with a deep sigh, saying, "I feel so bad for you. We also lost several relatives during the Holocaust in Poland, where my sister and I came from in 1932."

After a short pause, she continued, "My name is Dalia. I have a sister, Ronit, who recently lost her fiancé in a car accident, and she would like to meet a man. She is only twenty-three years old. Would you be interested? I assume that you are in good health, besides those scars that I have noticed."

She gave me her sister's address. (Most residents in those days had no phones in their homes.)

Ronit's address came in handy because the friends whom I had come with had relatives to stay with for one night, and I had nobody. One of my friends, Abrasha, offered me to stay with him at his relative's home. However, I was tempted to meet Ronit. I had to walk about eight blocks to get to the address that Dalia had given me. I knocked at the door and introduced myself. I was warmly welcomed. Ronit was a pretty young lady and very charming!

"I just came home from work, and I am going to eat supper. You are more than welcome to share a meal with me," Ronit said.

I could not resist the temptation to have a home-cooked meal in the company of a beautiful woman. Her manners and her fluent Hebrew made her feel like a *sabra* (a native).

She put me at ease right away by telling me, "You know my sister Dalia loves men and loves to be loved by them. Dalia believes that a woman should always be close to a man. She has been coaxing me to get one as soon as possible."

Ronit was deeply moved when I told her the tribulations I had endured during the war. With moist eyes, she leaned her face on my shoulder.

"Please do not cry. You have probably had enough grief and pain when your fiancé was killed. I do not wish to add to your burden," I said.

I did not dare to ask, but Ronit offered me to stay overnight on the sofa in her living room.

"You seem to be a gentleman, and I am sure that you will behave," Ronit said.

It turned out to be a romantic night. Ronit, three years my senior, said, "I just needed it. I hope we shall see each other often, and that you will be able to overcome all your emotional and financial problems. I am willing to help you as much as I can."

Our relationship lasted for two months. On one of my days off from kibbutz, Ronit took me to see Jerusalem, our ancient and holy city. Jerusalem was the epicenter for tourism while Tel-Aviv was the center of commerce and entertainment.

Ronit said to me, "We are making the desert bloom. Though our resources are limited, our dreams are limitless!"

I was very affected by Ronit's openhearted attitude towards me. Ours was a whirlwind romance, and it ceased sizzling when Ronit met Reuben, a thirty-year-old lawyer. He was well-established in the roots and culture of the Jewish community in Palestine. Soon after, Ronit married him, and I wished them both a happy union.

The Holocaust was then very much in Palestinian Jews' consciousness. Many people listened sympathetically to our horrific stories. After a while, they got tired and were no longer moved. Some let out a sigh, and some shed tears, but eventually they forgot. Such is life. People get used to everything. Sadly, they are willing to forget and must forget. Otherwise, it becomes difficult to breathe, to continue to live, and to take care of all the mundane tasks that ordinary life presents.

Occasionally, I spent time with other survivors who went through the same hell as I did. We discussed current events and our personal lives. Some managed to get jobs, to acquire skills, to settle in decent housing, to make friends, and to develop relationships with the opposite sex. Some regained their health, dressed well and even prospered. They demonstrated tremendous regenerative properties.

I wondered whether those present *Kazetnicks* (ex-prisoners), who a short time ago had been tortured and starving were for real. Were those the same eyes that saw the crematoriums? Were they the ones who were at the threshold of the gas chambers? Have they been trying to distance themselves from the hell they came from, to elude the bitter memories, and to stifle their cries? Did they prove that a strong spirit and a clear mind could restore their shattered lives and that they could be made happy again? Or, were they just keeping their pain hidden? Were those survivors an example for all Holocaust survivors to emulate? It looked to me like a collective amnesia.

Suddenly, I moved away, or they just left me. My face convulsed in pain and my eyes were burning. I was no longer among the liberated men. I was back in inimical death camps, hungry, and sick, waiting for the end of my life. The Nazi murderers were right behind me. I heard their barked-out orders, and their barking dogs. I heard voices pleading for help and for water but no one extended a hand. Nobody harkened to their last shrilly cry. Then I saw chimneys emitting smoke from ovens where my stepmother and my brothers, my relatives, my friends and so many other innocent people were burned.

I asked myself, "How did this happen that I am here? How could I have endured the humiliation, the starvation, and the physical and mental torture for thirty-five months of incarceration? I looked at myself, and I could not understand where I got my strength.

Was it my faith in the almighty God? It is written (in Aboth 4 and 11) that good deeds are a shield against retribution. My parents were righteous people, and as a youngster, I abided by their principles and beliefs. The Nazis deemed all of us to be inferior, but why did I survive and not my family? Why did I survive when millions of others perished? Most of them also had faith in God. Again, I could not find an answer!

MY UNCLE LOCATED ME

Menachem Tilles, my mother's brother, immigrated to Palestine in 1930 to escape poverty in Poland.

When World War II ended, everyone who had family or relatives in Europe were anxious to discover their fate. My uncle checked the list of people who had survived the concentration camps—the Jewish Agency and the Red Cross published the list intermittently. When he noticed my name among the survivors, and that I was "resettled" in the *kibbutz* Gan-Shmuel, he instantly came to take me to his home in Petah-Tiqvah.

As it turned out, I was the sole survivor of the entire Tilles family. The secretary and members of the kibbutz reacted lackadaisically to my leaving. They had wanted me to become a full-pledged member of the commune.

My uncle lived with his wife, Alta, and two school-aged daughters, Ruth and Yaffa, in a small house consisting of one living room, one bedroom, and an outhouse. I slept on the couch in the living room. My uncle worked in the agricultural dept of the *Histadruh* (workers union) for a moderate salary. I had no skills and I had no prospect of finding a well-paying job. My uncle's family shared with me what they could afford. In those days, almost everybody in Palestine struggled to make ends meet.

During the stay in my uncle's house, I did whatever menial work I could find. After several weeks, I moved into a one-room shack located in a citrus orchard. My furniture consisted of a futon, a folding metal table, two chairs, and an improvised closet of three empty wooden orange crates.

TWO MORE SURVIVORS

In Israel, I located two cousins, Dina and Ann, who also survived the Holocaust. Thus, six cousins, including myself, were the only remnants of our extended family of 128.

MY FIRST CLERICAL JOB

I got an entry-level clerical job at a canning company called "Yakhin." The woman-in-charge, Gusta, was at times very imperious. She used to dress me down for some small clerical errors. On the other hand, she was sympathetic to me as a Holocaust survivor. Many of her relatives in Poland also perished during the Holocaust. After five months it was February 17, 1948, and I was called to *Sheruth*-Haam (serve the nation).

SALUSIA

At the age of fourteen, Salusia was deported to Auschwitz (in 1944). She looked older than her actual age, so the Germans deemed her to be fit for work rather than to be liquidated, as most children her age were doomed to be. She was spared from the crematorium and liberated by the Russian Army, on January 27, 1945.

Salusia was born in Oświęcim (Auschwitz); and her parents were born in Chrzanów, my birthplace. I do not remember how we met, but I do remember how I adored her. She was a ravishing belle. She exuded radiant warmth with every chuckle and with every sigh. Her moral principals were the bedrock of her judgments. I would have gladly married her, but I could not abide by her practice of strict religious observance.

Sam, a schoolmate of mine, and also a Holocaust survivor, asked me in 1950, "Are you in a serious relationship with Salusia? If not, I am interested in her!"

I told him "Go ahead."

He did, and they have been happily married ever since. They live in Canada.

Petah-Tiqvah, Israel, January 18, 1948

MILITARY SERVICE IN ISRAEL

Three months before the establishment of the State of Israel, a busful of youngsters took us to Camp Dora, a military base in Nathanya that the British had vacated. We were taught clandestinely how to use firearms. I was soon classified as unfit to serve in a fighting unit. I was positioned in an administration unit where I ran errands at the base headquarters.

On May 15, 1948, the State of Israel was proclaimed. This was one of the most joyful moments in my life. A dream of millenniums had come to pass. The indomitable Jewish people regained their historic, eternal and inalienable right to *Eretz Yisrael*, the land of our forefathers. We had overcome all adversities in our struggle for survival and we had prevailed!

The military enabled soldiers and new immigrants to learn the Hebrew language by receiving study materials from the Military School for Education by Correspondence. Lessons and homework had to be mailed to the school for the teacher's review and then returned to the student/soldier.

Second Divisional Headquarters—October 1948.

A LETTER FROM A STRANGER

Once, I attached a personal note to the lessons which pertained to my situation. In response, I received a five-page handwritten letter from the chief administrator of the embryonic School by Correspondence. I was very surprised to receive a letter with philosophical implications. It was an injection of wit for me to ponder. The gesture and impact of that letter prompted me to include it in my memoirs. I am translating it from the Hebrew, to the best of my ability.

Tel-Aviv, February 21, 1949
Moshe Oster

Dear Colleague,

As the administrator of the Military School for Education by Correspondence, your personal note, which was attached to the lessons you mailed us, reached my desk. I am responding to your letter, not as a formal reply to your questions, but on a personal level, as man-to-man and soldier-to-soldier.

You might say that it is easy for a person who has not experienced life's travails to give advice. However, if you do pay attention to what I have to say to you, you might arrive at certain conclusions, which will reveal to you many things hidden in your soul of which you were not aware. Ordinarily, most individuals see and judge the other person, but it is difficult for the individual to see what is happening in his or her soul.

The fact that you entreat people that you do not know, and whom have never met you, is indicative that you have not lost faith in man. Despite your cruel fate, you do not complain against the world and humanity. This clearly shows that you are viscerally a healthy person, though you might not be physically healthy.

Since you have survived with a healthy mind, and you are so young, you are only twenty-two years old; the entire future is in front of you. You should not give up on life. It is true that you were terribly brutalized. I sympathize with you, as I do with the relatives of the six million Jews who were annihilated by a cruel murderer. However, our nation implores you—the past events belong to the past, and you have to start a completely new life.

I know that it is difficult! It is painful to think about all those dear relatives who are no longer here and to switch to a normal agenda as if nothing terrible had happened. It is difficult to forget the home of your father, the family togetherness, and those good days. There are two options in front of you. You can overcome your feelings and start to live, or you can sink in the abyss of degeneration. Your strong desire to learn proves that you have subconsciously decided to live and succeed. I am sure that you will choose the first path—the path of life. Once you have decided that this is your path, you will have no difficulties to go on. You have to remember, constantly, that man is born to live.

It is possible that a guilt feeling is brewing in your subconscious—a feeling that makes you ashamed that all your relatives were murdered while you were the only survivor of your entire family. This is the reason that you are saying, 'Regretfully, I survived.' However, since you are a remnant of a large and respected family, it is now your duty to continue the chain of your family and see to it that your family is, once again, a large and distinguished family. Destiny bequeaths to you that duty. It is a great mission. It is a responsible and respectful one, and you are obligated to carry it out. If you make it the purpose of your life, then you will feel that your very existence is not meaningless.

You are correct in stating that the most appropriate years for study—the school years—ages thirteen to eighteen, you were deprived of the freedom to pursue an education, and later on you were incarcerated in forced labor camps. However, have you ever heard that not many personalities throughout history had their beginnings wrapped in roses? Open a biography and you will see that only people forged in steel, who, at their beginnings suffered hunger, deprivation, and disabilities, reached greatness! It is a well-known fact that a person who grows without worries and is comfortable economically reaches, as the best scenario, mediocre levels. Most of the greatest inventors and the renowned started to get their education at a later age. They worked long hours under difficult circumstances. Their first experiments were conducted in primitive cellars or in poorly equipped workshops. A pampered person could not have endured those harsh conditions. Therefore, few pampered people reach the highest level of achievements. However, you, upon whom the cruel fate fell, have the foundation for a successful life. Perhaps you should be grateful that destiny put you in such position. Do not think about the plundered property or about the time wasted. Remember that property acquired by man can be lost at any time. The real property of man is his character. It is his quality that must be valued and appreciated.

Regarding the time that you were deprived of getting an appropriate education, do you know how many youngsters in our land dropped out of elementary school and went to work to enrich their education and knowledge in evening schools? Only a small percentage can afford the luxury of a comfortable college education, and you are going to be one of those who continues to study in the evenings. When you realize that you are not the only one who has to study in the evenings, you will no longer feel that you missed the chance to study.

Here, I would like to caution you not to make a mistake in your current situation. It is true that a person has to strive to enrich his knowledge. However, be careful not to make studies a substitute for life. There are times for learning, and there are times for a pastime. Everything is good and helpful if done in appropriate measure, and the same applies to learning. You will only see a blessing in your work if you devote a certain time for studies and some free time to exercise, social games, conversation with other soldiers, and learn to develop a relationship with the opposite sex. The scale of your soul will retain its balance. Only then will you be able to find real satisfaction in your studies. With the passing of time, you will realize that you had a worthy life.

A person was born to live in a society. If you distance yourself from socializing, you might be miserable all your life. However, if you choose to love your fellow man sincerely, and if you are willing to help anybody who needs your help (even though you might not be reciprocated for your help), and if you learn to love nature and the animals, then you may be assured of having a happy life. Do not think that happiness is possible only by wealth. Take a walk in the fields, and look at the green fields after the rain. Look at the birds that appear to have no worries. Look at the trees rattling in the wind. When you happen to be in a city, watch the people rushing and bustling; and listen to the pulse of the workers' toil. Go to the beach and watch the sunset or the waves hitting the shores. Wherever you observe the scenery well and the special characteristics of that site, then you will realize how lucky are the eyes that are able to see the beauty of the scenery. You have the ears that are able to listen to the chirping of the birds and to the rustle of leaves; and to the rushing flow of the ocean and rivers. Eventually, you will wish your legs to carry you on and on to see more and more. Then, you will feel the invigorated bloodstreams in your veins, eager to do something, to create moral, physical, and spiritual values that will last for eternity. If you choose this option, you will no longer say that you would like to devote most of your time to learning.

It is obviously worthwhile to make all the efforts to find a companion of the opposite sex. It is written in the Bible (Gen 2:18), "It is not good that the man should be alone." It is clear to me that a man at your age (and I understand it because I am only three years your senior) must feel a void if he has no female friend. It is understandable that being in the military makes it more difficult in this respect. However, there are many ways to find friendship even under these circumstances. One possibility is by correspondence. Put an ad in Bemachne (in camp), a weekly magazine issued by the military, that you are interested in corresponding with girls of your same age on different topics of interest to you. I am sure that you will receive responses, because there are many girls who are as lonely as you are. If you are sincere, fair, polite and kind, I am sure that an exchange of letters might lead to friendly ties and perhaps the binding of a lifetime. Remember that everybody feels lonely sometimes, and it is imperative for you not to sit with folded hands, but to meet people who are compatible with you.

If you reach these conclusions, you will realize that, besides knowledge and education which you cherish, and your love for nature, that companionship (especially with the opposite sex), has to be an integral part in the pursuit of a happy life. There are times for learning and times for playing; time to be serious and times to be jovial. If you have the stamina to persist in creative work and you succeed, then your studies will carry you step-by-step to a successful life.

When your wishes and requests fall on deaf ears, do not forget that each individual lives more or less in its own shell. Sometimes, the person that you are turning to may have serious problems, just as yours, and that person is not positioned to help. Do not despair, and do not give up hope! If you fail, try again persistently, and you will eventually succeed. When you arrived in this country, you were not able to attend Hebrew language classes. Now I am reading your well-written letter in Hebrew of which many natives would be proud. If you would not have mentioned in your letter that you were a new immigrant, and you had not taken any Hebrew lessons, I would have been sure that you had graduated from a school in this country. This fact is indicative that if you wish to accomplish something, and are willing to work hard, forgoing comfort in order to reach your goals, you will be able to. Here again, I have to caution you: Do not make your struggle for survival the purpose of your life—only as a means to reach the truthful goal. Remember, a person lives only one life, and if you do not utilize your days, every hour and every minute in order to get satisfaction from life, you might, with the passing of time, realize that you had struggled without knowing the purpose for your striving, and that you have not fulfilled your destiny.

As I have stated at the beginning of this letter, I had no intention to reply to the technical questions in your letter. I just wanted to encourage you and to make you aware of the mistakes that you might make in your present situation. If I succeeded, I shall feel rewarded.

Now, I am forwarding your letter to the teachers who will have to decide what educational material to send you.

Let me close, wishing you a successful future, as a free citizen, in a liberated land.—Moshe Oster

RINA

As a young child, Rina emigrated with her family from Turkey to Palestine. Rina and I developed a friendship while working in the same office of an army division's headquarters. It only took me a minute to fall in love with her. She swept me off my feet. Despite the striking difference between our cultural backgrounds, I was smitten with her indefinable beauty. Rina always had a smile on her face and a good word to say. Her pink baby cheeks projected an optimistic vivaciousness. She was as delicate as a flower, but she had an upright posture and an energetic demeanor. Her bright eyes saw life in bright colors. She was always dapper and relaxed, and there was a magic power in her calming voice. She never got annoyed. Rina had a way of looking at me that dazzled me. Her presence made me feel comfortable and lovable. She strove to comfort me. The war of independence was raging and the very survival of the nascent Jewish state was at stake. Rina granted me a respite from ominous peril; she was a scintillating spirit. The longer I knew her, the brighter her character shone in my eyes. Being in her presence was almost magically serene. Once I quoted to her Albert Einstein's theory of relativity, "Sit with a pretty girl for an hour, and it seems like a minute. That's relativity." I never had enough of Rina!

After several months of a sizzling hot relationship, we toyed with the idea of getting married when the war ended. However, her parents objected to the marriage, or even to dating an uneducated refugee from Europe—an Ashkenazi Jew. They insisted that she marry a Sephardic Jew, as all Jews from Turkey were. They also objected to me because I had no skills or money. Rina planned once to invite me to celebrate Passover with her family, but her parents discouraged her. We were both heartbroken. However, in her culture, a child never defied the parental wishes. Still, I shall forever remember Rina's warm embrace. She lightened the difficulties I faced in process of acclimatization in a new land of countless environmental and social challenges.

Not having a chance to tie our future together, we discontinued our relationship, but not our friendship—for as long as we both served in the army. It was extremely difficult to say good-bye when we were discharged from the service. Ten years later, I accidently met Rina on a bus. I was glad to hear that she had married a doctor who was a native of Turkey, and they had two beautiful children.

Rina and I, June 10, 1948.

DEBORAH

In May 1949, while I was still in the army, a sentry called the headquarters' office and asked for me. They told me that there was somebody at the gate to see me. I rushed to the gate and there she was. I just could not believe it! I was ecstatic and I trembled in her embrace. Deborah, whom I had met in D.P. camp Trophaiach in Austria, tearfully told me that she had been trying to locate me for over four years. She kept a diary during all those years about her feelings for me, along with her thoughts, and her longing to reach me and carry my family name. Finally, she located me by obtaining my address from a mail carrier at the Petah-Tiqvah post office. I felt like I was playing a role in a drama on a cinema screen, not just watching it.

Deborah and I in Israel on May 9, 1949.
It was the fourth anniversary of my liberation
from the concentration camp

We went out several times, and we were passionately in love. Deborah was anxious to get married, but I was not ready financially or emotionally.

Ten years later, I ran into Deborah in Tel-Aviv. By that time, she was a mother of five, and I was a father of a three-year-old boy.

ISRAEL'S WAR OF INDEPENDENCE

Despite all the difficulties and the imposed military regimentation, I was thrilled to witness the birth of an independent Jewish state—a haven for the persecuted, and a new home for many survivors of the Holocaust. The *Yishuv*—the 660,000 Jews—who had been living in Palestine during the Holocaust constituted the only entity on the globe that was willing to open its gates and arms for all Holocaust survivors.

The army became the most efficient melting pot for new immigrants. Many immigrants came from underdeveloped countries to blend into a nascent modern state. I could hardly stifle my emotions when the white and blue flag of Israel was raised in our base. Wherever this banner flutters today, my eyes glisten, and it stirs memories of centuries when it was just a dream. It was also the dream of many who perished in the Holocaust. I admired the phenomenal build-up of a country in its infancy. I have the highest reverence for *Zahal*, the Israeli Defense Forces who bravely stood as a strong barrier against those who were determined to destroy the remnants of the Jewish people. I pray that the Defense Forces of Israel will continue to withstand the enemies of Israel in spirit with David, Joshua, Maccabees, Bar-Kochba, the people of Masada, and the resisters of the Warsaw Ghetto.

The War of Independence put the nascent state of Israel deep in hock. Borrowing was necessary for the absorption of hundreds of thousands of new immigrants. Jews who had been dispersed around the globe came to the restored sovereign Jewish nation. Remnants of the Holocaust and Jews from over 100 countries, especially from Arab countries that were forced to flee, were streaming to Israel. There was an urgent need to procure weapons for the defense of the country. Consequently, interest rates went up, taxes were high, and the economic growth was slow. It was also very costly in blood. Six thousand soldiers lost their lives, which was about 1 percent of the Jewish population.

Thirty thousand were wounded. I wept when I met Josek Shapiro who lost a leg in the war. Josek was my older brother's best friend.

In November 1947, the Jewish Agency in Palestine accepted the Partition Plan adopted by the U.N. Resolution 181. The Arab counterparts did not. Not only did they reject it but also vowed to oppose it by force.

Azzam Pasha, the Secretary of the Arab League declared, **"This will be a war of extermination and a momentous massacre which will be spoken of like the Mongolian massacres and the Crusades."**

Arab riots erupted immediately in Palestine. As soon as Israel declared its independence, five Arab countries launched a "holy war of extermination to murder the Jews." The pro-Nazi **Grand Mufti** of Jerusalem, Amin el Husseini, who was a staunch admirer of Hitler, proclaimed, **"All Jews will be thrown into the sea."** The world just watched how the Jews, including many Holocaust survivors, were struggling to survive. The world was not concerned with the calling for the abolition of Israel. In the Middle East, hatreds are as ancient as the deserts. There are few oases. Israel became one of those oases, despite so many obstacles.

Today, Israel is being begrudged for turning a strip of arid land, of marshland and treeless mountains, into a blooming garden. A dot of undeveloped land morphed into a technological giant. It became a cultural beacon and a vibrant democracy in a sea of dictatorial states. Perhaps if Israel, a little pipsqueak country, would have oil in its ground, it would have been much better off. I remember seeing slogans on placards or scribbled on walls in Chrzanów, Poland, declaring, "*Żydostwo do Palestiny*, **Jews to Palestine!**" Now the Arabs, the Muslim world, the Jew-haters shout: **"Jews, go back where you came from. Get out of Palestine."** The Jews were there (1912 B.C.) before the Arabs, and when they trickled back in, they paid hefty prices for every parcel of land. Tragically, blind hatred transcends any just cause.

Had there been a Jewish state during World War II, the gates would have been wide open for hundreds of thousands of refugees who were not let in by other countries, including the U.S. and Britain. Disasters like the loss of the "Struma"—769 Jews from Eastern Europe attempted to flee to Palestine on board the Struma. However, instead of finding freedom, they found a world that didn't want to give them shelter—a world that cast them out, defenseless, into the raging seas—could have been avoided. Now, when we refuse to be led like sheep to the slaughter, as the Nazis led six million Jews, the cynical world is not pleased!

After eight months of service in the army, my Hebrew improved and I was able to carry out office procedures more efficiently. The officer-in-charge was pleased with my performance and I was promoted to corporal. Three months later, I was promoted to sergeant. The officer-in-charge, Eli, and I developed a friendly relationship that lasted for years after both of us were no longer in the army. The document below states that I, Sergeant Alter Wiener, have served, from March 15, 1948 to June 15, 1949 in the headquarters of the Second Division. I have proven my loyalty, extraordinary dedication, talent, ability, and efficiency in every designated duty.

I was pleased to get so far. I deplored the fact that my parents and my family could not read this. **Every instance of satisfaction or joy has been overshadowed by sadness, stemming from events during the Holocaust.**

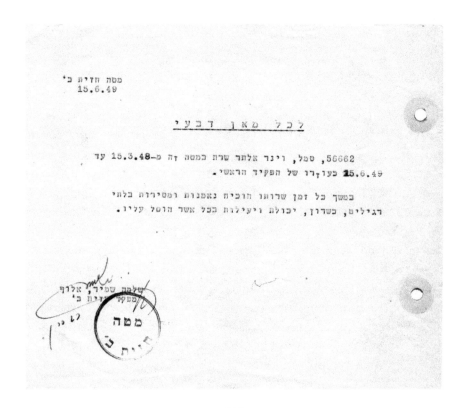

I BECAME A CIVILIAN AGAIN

After my release from the army, I returned to my clerical job at Yakhin, where I had worked before joining Service the Nation. (Employers were required to rehire their veteran- employees.)

Gusta was still working at Yakhin and she granted me a position in the bookkeeping department. As a trainee, I received a small salary. It was difficult to eke out a living. I could not afford to live comfortably and spend much on dating girls. Gusta was fully aware of that. To make me feel better, or to make me work harder, she daily treated me to cake that she had baked. I was content with having a sedentary job and prospects for acquiring a profession. Gusta was pleased with the progress I had made in the basic principals of bookkeeping and my work habits.

One day, while making bookkeeping entries, Gusta kissed me and asked, "How are you going to post the kiss I gave you? Will you debit or credit my account?"

My heart was racing to my throat. I got bamboozled! The question stumped me.

She continued, "I taught you that the golden rule of bookkeeping is the one who gives, his account is being credited; and the one who receives, his account is being debited."

She went back to her desk with a big smile, and left me in a daze. The following day, once again, Gusta approached me from behind, ostensibly to show me how to post a certain transaction. Then, her kiss landed on my lips. I was not comfortable with her provocative advance. Gusta was married, had no children, and lived in Tel-Aviv, where she enjoyed a relatively comfortable life.

Gusta proved that despite her unattractive face, she was able to get a man, twenty-four years her junior. I could not afford to quit the job, because I badly needed the salary to survive. Those were very difficult times and unemployment was rampant. Prevalent austerity affected everybody's standard of living. Food and everything else was rationed.

When Gusta gave me a bar of chocolate, a luxury in those days, she said, "I am giving it to because chocolate is an aphrodisiac."

Gusta asked me to visit her at her apartment. She wanted to introduce me to her husband. I graciously accepted her invitation.

When I rang her bell, Gusta opened the door wearing a nightgown. Instead of introducing me to her husband, she introduced me to her bedroom. I was befuddled. It did not take long to be seduced. I liked the seduction but not the trick.

"Intimacy is the glue that holds a marriage together, and I don't have enough of it; you came in handy," Gusta said.

I felt that my job would be in jeopardy if I did not cooperate fully with Gusta. Although Gusta was a flame, her wile somehow spooked me, and I quit Yakhin in October 1950.

In October 1950, I got a job at Emile Visser & F. Shiller Ltd., an export company of citrus fruits in Tel-Aviv. My job was to write orders from individuals who came to our office to purchase a gift box of oranges to be shipped to relatives or friends in Europe. This precious commodity was not available, then, in any of the East European countries under communism.

I recall a woman showing me a letter she had received from her sister in Prague, Czechoslovakia. It stated that a doctor told her that only oranges could help her to recover from a certain disease. It was interesting to learn that so many Israeli residents, who themselves faced scarcity in basic food staples, were in a position to help others. This was a seasonal job.

In September 1951, I was rehired by Yakhin. Gusta, my seducer, was no longer there. Still, lacking professional skills, I did all kinds of clerical work that didn't satisfy my intellectual needs. I left Yakhin in November 1958.

MARRIAGE

I met Esther in March 1951, at my uncle's home. She paid a casual visit when I happened to be there. Since most people had no telephones in those days, it was acceptable for a friend or neighbor to drop by without prior notice.

Esther showed interest in my life story. She lived with her parents across the street from my uncle's house. After a long chat, she said, "I would like you to meet my parents. They are also from Poland, and have lost many of their relatives in the Holocaust. You will have a lot to talk about."

Appealing to Gusta in Tel-Aviv on August 4, 1950

Esther's elderly parents welcomed me warmly, and I stayed for a while. On my way out, Esther and her parents said, "Nice meeting you, *LeHitraot*" (see you again).

Since I got out from the army, I had close relationships with women. I was not chaste but did not consider any of them to be in a relationship that could have led to marriage. I just was neither ready financially nor fit emotionally to make a matrimonial commitment and eventually have children. I had been troubled by the thought that bringing children into a world where they could suffer as I did would be irresponsible. Flashback of atrocities I experienced in the Holocaust never ceased to ferment in me.

Esther and I did go out for several months. We liked each other, although we came from two different worlds. Esther was a native of Palestine, a *"sabra"*—referring metaphorically to a cactus with a prickly exterior and tender inside. She did not experience the persecution that I did, and she was educated—a kindergarten teacher. I admired her talents in drawing, painting, and sculpturing. It made me feel good, proud, and lucky to be in a relationship with a person of such caliber. Esther had parents, two brothers and other close relatives. Many friends from her early childhood and school peers surrounded her. I had no home, no parents, no siblings, no education, no profession, no property, and no decent income. Her friends wondered and questioned her why she would get involved with a new immigrant, an orphan, and a Holocaust survivor with baggage and emotional problems. They saw me as an alien to the pioneer spirit of most Israelis.

The Israeli old-timers were compassionate and helpful, but they saw the Holocaust survivors as miserable wretches who let the Nazis shove them into the crematoriums instead of organizing and fighting back. I was told once, "You were not only cowards but masochists." My explanation about how impossible it was to resist was barely palatable to the *Sabras*. They looked down at me. Esther listened to the dictates of her heart. She liked my good looks, my European manners, my tenderness, and my eagerness to acquire knowledge. I was different. I was not as abrasive as the young men she knew. I was the antithesis of the sharp-tongued Israeli-born *sabras*.

Of all my Holocaust survivor friends, only one married a non-survivor. Most survivors realized that only another survivor could be an empathetic spouse.

At that time, Esther's parents were aware of an ongoing affair between Esther and Peretz, who was a married man. They were anxious to untangle their daughter from a precarious situation, and apparently felt that I might be the catalyst to putting an end to that relationship.

I was invited for dinner on Friday nights and became a frequent visitor. To have a cooked meal at a family table was a rare occasion—something I missed for the last ten years. At that time, I lived in a rented room in a family's apartment, where I had no access to a kitchen. There were very few restaurants in Petah-Tiqva, and I could not afford to dine there anyway. Every visit with her family, the Golombs, was a real treat for me. It was a re-introduction to a normal family environment. I had been deprived of this aura and aroma for many years.

As our relationship deepened, Esther's affair with Peretz ended. At the heat of romance Esther said, "I can see how you miss your family. I can hear your nightmarish dreams. I promise you that I will fill in for your lost family. I shall shower you with a love that will sprout sweet dreams."

When my inner voice asked me whether I wanted to be married, my answer was no. I felt an aching gap. Post-traumatic stress of the Holocaust lingered on within me. I was very reluctant to get married, but I did. I did not make the right decision but I tried for years to make the decision right.

The text of the wedding invitation cards read, "Chaim and Chaya Golomb have the honor of inviting you to the wedding of their daughter, Esther, to Alter Wiener, the son of the **late** Pearl and Mordechai."

To be a young groom and an orphan startled many invitees and interjected a sad thought of a joyful event.

Despite her good intentions, Esther did not fulfill her promises. She was just unable to deliver the emotional support of which I was in dire need. Esther had difficulties comprehending that my actions and inactions were somehow connected with my traumatic past. It was a heavy load that I carried at all times. She invalidated many of my perceptions that were formulated in the world which I came

Our wedding day, March 19, 1952

from. Marriage per se is not an easy institution. My emotional load generated marital problems.

I pleaded with Esther not to raise her voice, and not to shout, because it reawakened traumatic memories from the concentration camp. Hearing a child crying reminded me of how babies and small children were crying when they were forcefully separated from their mother and deported. At the slightest noise, I impulsively raised my hands to protect my face from expected punches and conks. Esther's insensitivity to my past was hurting me. She could not see my bleeding heart.

Garrulous Esther had a habit of telling her friends about my shortcomings. She sometimes made vitriolic remarks to castigate me in front of our children and in front of our friends for any trivial thing that I had unwittingly done to her disliking. Her scathing opinions

One year after the wedding

about me, justified or not, drilled into the core of my self-esteem. I had lived with the stigma of being inferior for a long time, and I expected my spouse to invalidate that stigma.

Her parents let us live in one room of their house. It was the same room that Esther had lived in prior to our marriage. While planning the wedding, her father promised to build a second floor on top of his house for us. After the wedding, there was a start—several walls were erected, but nothing else. Apparently, her parents did not have the financial resources to complete the structure. I obviously resented the fact that they had not kept their promise. I wondered if the unrealistic commitment was made to lure me into the marriage to extricate Esther from her affair with a married man.

After several months, we took a big mortgage and moved into a one-bedroom condo with a small living room and microscopic-sized kitchen. It might sound very modest, but for me, it was a luxury.

In June 1969, Esther left for Israel with both children, to help care for her aging and sickly parents. I had no objection because I believed that it was her moral duty. We also hoped that a temporary separation would be beneficial to both of us. In June 1970, she rejoined me in the U.S. Esther made twenty-two trips to Israel between 1961 and 1982. She stopped traveling when both parents passed away.

In 1982, Esther was diagnosed with Parkinson Disease. She has been in a nursing home for the last several years.

MORDECHAI (MARTIN)

Our first child was born on October 9, 1956. It was a gift for my thirtieth birthday. He bears my father's name. I was glad that the name of a family branch, cut off by the Nazis, would grow again. Moty, our son's nickname, came at a time when my army reserve unit was mobilized to take part in the "Sinai Campaign." In 1956, Israel was at war with Egypt. Esther's stay in the hospital was shortened to make room for the war casualties.

In October 1969, on Saturday, at the local synagogue in Israel, Martin celebrated his Bar Mitzvah. When he recited the *Haftarah* (a chapter from the Prophets), it evoked my emotions. At the time of my scheduled Bar Mitzvah, we were mourning the murder of our beloved father. I was deprived of a significant milestone in a young Jewish boy's life. Bar Mitzvahs were not festive occasions, as practiced now. Rather, they were religious rituals that took place in the sanctuary instead of in a catering hall.

I probably was not an ideal father, because I could never please him as much as I had tried. I gave him everything that he needed but not always what he wanted. My cherished values and my life story were blasé for Moty.

He once told me, "You are dwelling too much on the Holocaust."

He did not understand that I was not able to swaddle my pain and encase the feelings.

From his early childhood on, he let me have an implicit message, "Talk all you want but I shall do all I want."

Citing the fifth commandment, "Honor your father and mother so that you may live long" fell on deaf ears. My wife was utterly tuned into our son's desires but not to his obligations. I believe that when children do not have an authority figure at home, it makes them feel insecure.

Moty married Elaine Guttman in 1982 and they have four beautiful children. I disagree with my children's philosophy and their lifestyle, but I never questioned their right to be wrong. My love for all of them will never diminish, even when I deem their attitude towards me not to be as respectful as I understand it should be.

ALEXANDROWITZ

In November 1958, I responded to an ad for a bookkeeping job at Alexandrovitz, a wholesaler of rubber goods in downtown Tel-Aviv. The man who preceded me had a heart attack and died at his desk. This was an office operated by one person, and there was nobody else who was able to facilitate the transition, and to hand over the paperwork.

I put an ad in the newspaper for an assistant bookkeeper, and Nurit, who was seventeen years old applied for the job. When I interviewed her, I learned that her family, along with many other Jewish people, were compelled to get out of Iraq in 1951. They left most of their possessions behind. Those refugees settled in Israel where they found shelter in *ma'abaroth* (transit camps). There were seven daughters and two sons in Nurit's family. She was an attractive young girl with black hair, brown eyes, and an exotic appearance. She had a healthy insight and charming demeanor. As reflected in other chapters, I had

Nurit, once my assistant bookkeeper, is a dear friend for eternity.

been deprived of basic human rights for so many years. When I was incarcerated in concentration camps during the Holocaust, I made a vow to myself that if I would ever become a free man, I would be compassionate. I vowed to be the antidote to the poisonous travails to which I was subjected. I would walk in the path of love, not hate, and I would share the fruits of my labor. My suffering made me sensitive to others' misfortunes.

I hired Nurit, although she had absolutely no prior clerical experience. I empathized with her, because I was full of gratitude to have an opportunity to reach out and to be able to exercise kindness. I made a difference in a young girl's life, and I helped a beautiful, innocent soul to a more promising future by training her in secretarial duties.

Like the Biblical Samuel, I said to myself, "May the Lord reward me according to my righteousness." To share with others what you have learned is the highest call of Judaism. My investment in Nurit's professional development appreciated. She was a quick learner and an excellent co-worker. We became good friends and have been ever since. Nurit has always addressed me as *boss yakiri* (my dear boss), and never as Mr. Wiener. When I gave her a little gift for her eighteenth birthday, she was overwhelmed.

"This is the first time in my life that somebody gave me a gift on my birthday," she uttered with moist eyes.

Nurit was very naïve and did not know how to thank me appropriately. Hugs were uncommon in those days, so she bit my arm to release her emotions. Nurit and her husband, Shaul, have been living in the USA since 1984. They have four beautiful children and twelve grandchildren. I am thankful and humbled to know that Nurit acquired a profession with my help, and our friendship is everlasting. Nurit was imbued with a sense of compassion, and I glow in her accomplishments. I remember vividly when she accommodated her sick uncle in her small apartment, in Chulon, Israel. She took care of him until he died. She did this while rearing, with full devotion, her own small children. These are values that I had cherished then, and I still do!

I left Alexandrovitz in September 1960 for the USA.

EMIGRATION

I lived in Israel for fourteen years. I paved roads, tilled and irrigated arid soil, planted trees, picked oranges, cleaned toilets, and served in the Israeli army. I learned the Hebrew language, office work, and bookkeeping. I made many friends and got married.

Israel, with a population of about two million in the early '50s was surrounded by five hostile Arab countries with a population of over 100 million. There were daily incursions from across the borders leading to clashes and casualties. I had to serve in the army reserves at least one month every year. After all the travails that I faced during World War II, and the year of wandering in Europe as a displaced person, the absorption hurdles as a refugee in Palestine/Israel sapped my physical and mental strength.

My physician told me that I must have a respite from the constant tension to which I had been subjected for so long. He propounded that it would be psychologically helpful to leave Israel and reside, at least for several years, in a country free of conflict or social upheaval. Tranquility was imperative for my diagnosed psychoneurosis not to worsen.

In 1953, I applied at the U.S. consulate for a visa. My cousin, Kossek, in the U.S.A. sponsored me. He assured the U.S. Immigration officials that I would not become a financial burden to the American taxpayer. After seven years of anticipation, the American Consulate notified me that my application had been approved under the Polish Quota. The letter from the consulate stated that if I did not leave within a certain time, my chances to go to the U.S. would be forfeited. I did not want to lose that opportunity, and I left on September 27, 1960 by "Zion," an Israeli ship. Esther preferred to "wait and see" how I would manage in the U.S. We sold our condo, and she moved with our son into her parents' house.

MY LIFE IN THE USA—
ENCHANTED BY FREEDOM AND OPPORTUNITY

Upon debarking on October 10, 1960, my cousin Benny and his wife, Evelyn, welcomed me at the New York Port. I stayed in my cousin's apartment for several weeks.

While still on the ship, I received a telegram from Esther advising me that she had decided to join me. She and our son came by air four weeks after my arrival in the U.S. We moved into a two-bedroom apartment at 1620 St. Johns Place in Brooklyn. Having no skills and knowing very little English, I could only find drudged work. I went to school in the evenings. I graduated from elementary school at the age of thirty-five, and I graduated from high school with an Equivalency Diploma at the age of thirty-six.

In January 1961, we moved to 506 Eastern Parkway in Brooklyn. Later, we moved to 377 Montgomery Street. We were compelled to

Board of Education
of the City of New York
ALTER WIENER

Has satisfactorily completed the course of study for Evening Elementary Schools has earned the approbation of the principal and teachers and is entitled to pursue an Evening High School course in The City of New York

In Testimony Whereof we have affixed our signatures

hereto this   23rd   day of May   19 61

President Board of Education

John J. Theobald
Superintendent of Schools

Evening Elementary School 167

Borough of Brooklyn

Mark E. _____
Teacher-in-Charge

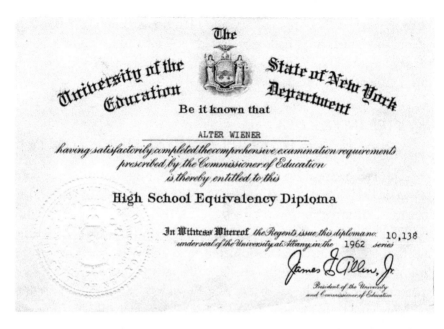

change locations because of the drug-ridden neighborhoods. Crime was rampant. I was mugged twice, but I could not afford to move to a much better or safer neighborhood or to any other borough or suburb of New York City. Still, I just thought how fortunate I was to live in the U.S.A.

BIRNABUM BROS. INC.

I was constantly looking for a better paying and more intellectually stimulating job. In August 1961, I noticed a "Help wanted" ad for a bookkeeper position. I had some bookkeeping experience from Israel, but I was unfamiliar with the bookkeeping system and the pertinent vernacular in the U.S. Being told that New York air smacks of opportunities, I asked for an appointment. They gave me an employment application form to be completed. I was in a quandary when I reached the question about my formal education. Since I had hardly completed any schooling, I wrote under the column of "Names of Schools Graduated," the following: Blechhammer, Brande, Gross-Masselwitz, Klettendorf and Waldenburg.

Robert Birnbaum, one of the owners who had reviewed the application, said to me, "I have never heard about these learning institutions."

I became quite jittery, and embarrassingly replied, "These are the five forced labor camps in Germany where I spent my school years."

Mr. Birnbaum was taken aback and speechless. After consulting with his brothers and partners, Mr. Brirnbaum called me in and said, "Because of your honesty and our sympathy for your past, we are willing to hire you on a trial basis as of August 1, 1961. The weekly salary will be $55.00."

This was a real plum. It was the best news that I had received in a long time.

The company was desperate to get somebody to run the office, which consisted of a head bookkeeper and four clerks. The head bookkeeper went out for lunch and never came back. She even left her slippers under her desk. Later on, we heard that she had been hospitalized for some mental problems.

My bosses treated me with respect and our employer/employee relationship gradually evolved into a mutual friendship of common concern for the health of the business and our personal well-being. I felt appreciated by all three owners and their respective families. In February 1963, my bosses left a flight ticket and a paid receipt for a reserved hotel room in Florida, on my desk with a note, signed by all partners. It read, "Dear Al, Spend a nice vacation, your first one in the U.S.A., at our expense. We appreciate your dedication to the job."

I attended Brooklyn College in the evenings, but regretfully I did not have a chance to graduate. I did however, complete courses in accounting, insurance, and commercial law. It was exhausting to work all day for a meager livelihood and study in the evening to acquire a vocation. Unfortunately, I have not met anybody who likes to pay taxes, which was an integral part of my accounting practice. I saw no smile on a client's face when I handled him a prepared tax return.

Even though accounting has been my time-consuming occupation, I cannot state that it has been my major life's work or pastime. I am an autodidact. I had to teach myself what I could not be taught in a class.

Eventually, I became the controller of Birnbaum Bros., Inc. I was entrusted with a position that had exceeded my most ambitious hopes. That position provided a decent sustenance for my family. The recognition of my contribution and being accorded a respectful status counteracted the adversities and humiliations attributed to my *untermentch* (subhuman) characterization during my teenaged years.

The Birnbaums and I conversed on a horizontal level—the antidote to a vertical, top-down monologue, typical in an employer and employee environment. I had never been "bossed" by any of the three brothers/ bosses. I felt a strong emotional attachment to that place and its owners. They embraced me with love, and only the death of Robert Birnbaum separated me from them after twenty years of engagement.

RON

Our second child was born in 1964. It was Esther's wish to have another child, a brother for Martin. Ron was a source of joy. The sharpness of Ron's observations and his keen analytical mind were remarkable from an early age.

In June 1973, we celebrated Ron's Bar Mitzvah in a synagogue in Forest Hills, New York. Many of our friends and Ron's schoolmates took part in the celebration.

The older I get, I am more appreciative of my parents' guidance and teachings. I was brought up not to question parents' dictates or tactics, though they probably made missteps, as all humans do. Ron, however, has a compelling desire to jettison my values from the "old country." He walks in the path of his contemporaries.

I understand that it is important to let my children know their ancestral roots, but Ron has no interest to know. He relates condescendingly towards me, perhaps of his technological sophistication and financial successes in comparison to mine. Ron, like many others of his generation, thinks that he is culturally superior to his father's generation. I sense an unbearable frustration when he swims away from my embrace. Apparently, it is all part of *tsar gidul banim* (the grief of raising sons/children).

I recognize that I had inhabited a very different world than Ron does. With the passing of time, he may be eager to search for the roots that shaped my constitution and are dear to me, and presently alien to him. There is an old African adage, "When an old man or an old woman dies, the village loses a library, because of the wealth of knowledge and information that they were able to share." Such loss definitely occurs when a parent passes away. "Sit before your parents and the elders and learn from them. Sit amid the dust of their feet; follow them and study under them." (Aboth1,4)

I have also learned that children must respect their parents. Children have an obligation to care for their elderly parents. I always remember my parents caring for their parents. My father said once, "I derive happiness by fulfilling my duty of *Kibud Horim* (respect/caring for our parents)." Today, regretfully, that tenet is rarely observed. It is a painful reality for those in the last phase of their lives.

Ron is married to Doreen Kiss, a pediatrician. They have two adorable boys. I love them dearly as I love their parents.

CITIZENSHIP

On March 1, 1966, we became U.S. citizens, which was an important milestone in my life. I have always admired this land of freedom and opportunity. On this occasion, our older son changed his name from Mordechai to Martin, a more common name, easier to spell and pronounce.

MY BROTHER SHMUEL'S FATE

Since my brother Shmuel did not show up after the war, I presumed that he had perished in one of the camps. In 1990, at a New York gathering of Holocaust survivors from our town, a man approached me saying, "You don't know me, but I remember you as a little boy. I was the bookkeeper in your father's business." He continued," I have to tell you something very sad, but it is imperative for you to know. I was in Auschwitz. At one point, my job was to push victims into the gas chambers and another time to shove the victims into the crematorium. I knew an inmate who recognized his naked wife on the way to the gas chamber. I am sorry to tell you that I, with my own hands, pushed your brother, Shmuel, into the gas chambers. I knew him well."

Thus, I learned that my brother was murdered in Auschwitz. I do not know the exact date of his demise.

ISRAM TRAVEL AND RAFAELLA SPORTSWEAR

I was the controller for Isram Travel from June 1980 until July 1981, and from then until April 2000, I was the controller for Rafaella Sportswear, Inc.

In April 2000, I retired and moved to Hillsboro, Oregon, where my son Ron had been living for ten years. Ron urged us to move to Oregon. He promised to be helpful and supportive in every possible way. What was especially important was that he had promised to take care of his mother, inflicted with a progressive Parkinson disease. I was very reluctant to leave New York for Oregon, but Esther decided to move. I had no choice but to go along. She always got her way.

SHARING MY LIFE STORY— SOME NOTEWORTHY RESPONSES

As stated in the preface of this book, I have been sharing my life story for the last six years. My audiences are students in middle school, high school and college. I also speak to church congregants of denominations, synagogues, and prisons for young and adult offenders in the states of Oregon and Washington.

To this date, I have received thousands of letters from those who have heard me, and I am reproducing some noteworthy responses.

11/27/00—CENTURY HIGH SCHOOL, HILLSBORO, OREGON

I was quite nervous and apprehensive whether my speech would be well received by a class of juniors. This was the first time in my life that I spoke to any audience.

Erica, the teacher, was very friendly and made sure that her students were respectful, and indeed they behaved well and most listened raptly to my life story.

I opened my speech by saying, "I am not a jealous person, but I cannot avoid a twinge of envy seeing you in school. I, at your age, was not so privileged. The Germans forbade me to attend school and therefore my formal education ended at the age of thirteen. I was disturbed to read in this morning's paper that in the state of Oregon, one out of four high school students drops out. It is a pity that so many do not know how to appreciate the chance of getting a free education."

I received a thank you card signed by all students. About a year later, I stepped into a shoe store. A young girl approached me saying, "May I help you?"

"Yes, please," I said.

Then, taken aback, she exclaimed, "I know you. You are Al Wiener, and you spoke at my class about a year ago."

I told her that I was glad that she had recognized me.

The girl continued, "You know my mother would like to hug and kiss you!"

"I am ready at any time to allow that to happen," I said.

"But you don't know why," she said.

I did not particularly care why. "One is never too old for that," I retorted.

"Well, I'll tell you why. At the time when you spoke at Century High, I was considering dropping out of school, but then listening to your story and how you were forbidden to attend school at the age of thirteen, I realized that I am indeed lucky. I told my mom that I should continue school and work here part-time. My mom would like to express her appreciation to you for making her daughter stay in school."

1/26/01—SWEET HOME HIGH SCHOOL, SWEET HOME, OREGON

Carol had often come to see her mother at Rosewood Park Assisted Living, where I was a resident at that time. One day, I told Carol how much I admired the care and love she had shown for her mother. When Carol noticed my accent, she asked me which country I had come from.

When I told her that I was a Holocaust survivor from Poland, her eyes moistened and she said, "I just came back from a visit to Auschwitz."

She embraced me and wept while relaying the impact Auschwitz had on her and her family.

She continued, "The traces of the horrors that took place in Auschwitz-Birkenau were difficult to view and to comprehend how men could be so cruel to their fellow man."

Several weeks later, Carol invited me to share my story with her students at Sweet Home High School. I received eighty-six letters, expressing sympathy and deep respect. Below, is a letter from one teacher.

Jan. 31, 2001

Dear Mr. Weiner,
My name is Jennifer Davis; I was at Sweet Home High School when you visited and spoke last week. I was the Jennifer who approached you to tell you about my parents knowing Holocaust survivors and instead started to cry. I have taught in Sweet Home for 5 years, and I have had many memorable experiences. But perhaps the most memorable was you. I write poetry once in a while, especially when I am touched by something. I wrote this one for you:

Mysterious Ways

As a little girl,
I sat in church...
    foreboding organ music,
    priests in grassy green robes,
    arms up high lifting the word of God on high.
I would stare at Jesus on the cross,
and wonder what he went through,
nailed to a cross?
I never understood suffering.
    "God has a reason..."
    "God works in mysterious ways."
Was what they told me, when I would ask,
and I believed it...I knew it was true.
I still do.

And so...
A small, beautiful eye he had
a horrible story he told,
a wonderful outlook on life,
a commitment to life, family,
to his message he brought.
It was him as Him...
God brought him to me.
He came to speak about tolerance, education,
And his message was clear to me,
As clear as God in the eyes of my children,
for I know he is there too.

Thank you...thank you for
your spirit, it has lifted me to new levels
Thank you...thank you for
your story, it has touched my inner soul
Thank you...thank you for
your message, it will be carried wherever I go.

The little girl in me still wonders
about suffering,
still wants to know why?
and however paradoxical as it is,
it remains a
mysterious way.   *-Jennifer Davis (1-30-01)*

I am a catholic and it has always been told to me that "God works in mysterious ways." This phrase has baffled me for years, as I am sure it has you too. What happened last Friday is one of those ways, those mysteries.

I am writing you to thank you for being God in my life...for representing that mysterious way. I know that there was a reason that I approached Carol Fleenor casually before school just to have a few friendly words with an adult before the masses of teenagers took over my life, and that reason was you, for it was then that Carol invited me to hear you speak. I thought, "Oh...cool...I'll take my whole class; it will be interesting." Well, interesting does not describe the feelings that came over me as you spoke. Love for human beings, sorrow for suffering, bitterness at those who hate, an eternal nagging in my gut saying...WHY? is what came over me...it was never interesting at all.

Thank you for your kindness...for your loving eyes. For your willingness to share your story with me, with us. Thank you for the message of tolerance and education. Thank you for the loving touch you gave me when I cried.

I promise that I will read The Sunflower and let you know what I think of it. I am forever touched by you, and I feel your visit was one that was meant to happen for me.

Your friend,

Jennifer L. Davis
Jennifer Davis

1/28/01—PORTLAND CABLE ACCESS (CHANNEL 11) PORTLAND, OREGON

I have never dreamt that I would appear before a live audience at a TV station. The interview lasted for over an hour and was aired in 2001 on February 13, February 17, February 18, February 20, and February 28. I have been told that hundreds of thousands of Oregonians have seen reruns of that taped program ever since.

2/20/01—VALLEY CATHOLIC SCHOOL, BEAVERTON, OREGON

I was warmly received by the teacher and the students. This phenomenon for me was very uplifting, because as a student in a public

132

elementary school in Poland, I was sometimes taunted by my Catholic peers. I appreciated that religious tolerance was indeed prevailing in this land of a diverse populace.

2/27/01—BARNES ELEMENTARY SCHOOL, KELSO, WASHINGTON

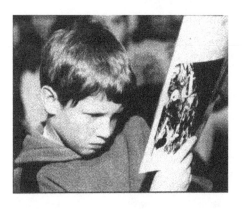

I questioned the teacher, Lisa, whether it would be proper to use the same graphic language in presenting my story of horrors to her eleven-year-old students as I do with older students. I was concerned that horrific details might rob the kids of their sleep.

Her response was, "Today's kids watch television and are familiar with violent scenes. They have to learn about the Holocaust and listen to the personal experience of Holocaust victims as long as there are survivors alive."

Students got an up-close look, in words and pictures, at the horrors of Hitler's concentration camps during Kelso's Holocaust assembly.

Courtesy of the Washington Education Association

4/19/01—OREGON STATE UNIVERSITY, CORVALLIS, OREGON

The program, "OSU Holocaust Memorial Week 2001" was well attended by students and members of the Corvallis community. Many in the audience of about 800 were moved to tears while listening to the horrors I was subjected to during the Holocaust.

At the conclusion of my presentation, I was approached by about 100 students with more questions. They showed a keen interest in all the ramifications of my suffering during and after the Holocaust and the relevancy to their own life.

One letter from a student is reproduced below.

Dear Mr. Weiner,

Tonight you spoke at Oregon State University and I was in the audience. I wish to thank you with all that I am for what you do, for who you are. I wish to express my admiration for your love, for your understanding, for your gift to us all. Every time you speak to us, every time you share your understanding, it is an honor to us all.

You have touched my life, dear sir. As a sculptor touches clay, you have molded a part of me. As light touches the leaves, you have given me the strength to grow. For these things, I know not how to thank you. For these are gifts beyond value.

You took me back to Poland. I was there nine years ago. You reminded me simultaneously of two experiences I had there. One was a visit to a graveyard. The emotions of sorrow and pain, of loss and isolation took me there. I was a younger boy then, as hurt then as I am now by those whose voices are silent. And yet, at the same time, you reminded me of riding on a train through the forests near Warsaw. The sun was setting through the clouds as they burst with rain. And thus the sun's rays broke through the clouds in beams of glowing light as we raced through the trees.

You have reminded me that as much pain, sorrow, and horror that exist in the world, there is even more love, kindness, and hope. I hope that I can remember this hope and this love in my heart. For even now there is so much suffering in the world. I will not give up though. You have inspired me to help heal those injured, and to remember that blame is never a solution.

You have shared such gifts with me, and I am sure many others. I wish I could give such a gift, even a shadow of such a gift, back to you. With my hands empty, I can give you my love, my respect, and my hope.

Good luck and good health to you and your family, always. May your lessons of love and understanding inspire others to love each other.

Sincerely,

4/20/01—HILLEL FRATERNITY GROUP, EUGENE, OREGON

The audience of diverse ethnicity and age was very attentive.

One student whom I had noticed was not at ease during my speech said to me, after my presentation, "I felt like walking out but my girl friend held me back."

"Why?" I asked him.

"Well, my grandfather took part in atrocities committed in Poland, and listening to you I just had a terrible guilt feeling."

"You are not responsible for your grandfather's actions and I have nothing against you. In fact, you and I could be the best of friends." I said.

Our discussion continued for a while, and then I said to him, "I wouldn't feel comfortable to shake hands with your grandfather, if he would be here, but with you, I have no problem."

We shook hands and parted amicably.

An older lady approached me, saying, "Thank you so much for sharing your story with us. It must have been very painful to you. I do have a request. I am going home now and would like to relay your message to my daughter. Could you please summarize it for me?"

"Yes, I can do it in one sentence. Love your neighbor as yourself (Lev.18, 19). Hillel (that this fraternity is named in his honor), a famous rabbi in Talmudic times (30 B.C.) who headed a *yeshiva* (a house of study) said, "Do not do unto others what you would not have done to you. All the rest, he said, is commentary."

4/20/01—"TEACHING THE HOLOCAUST: A DIALOGUE ACROSS THE DISCIPLINES"

The program took place in Willamette University in Salem, Oregon. Twenty teachers from the states of Oregon and Washington participated in that seminar, led by Dr. Bill S. and Dr. Mike S. I was asked to share my Holocaust experience with those teachers. The coordinator of the speakers at OHRC introduced me, and in my opening remarks, I said, "I feel honored to speak to you and share with you my experience during the Holocaust so that you may convey the lessons to your students. I am not an educated person as you all are; my formal schooling ended at the age of thirteen. I have never dreamt to be so privileged to speak to such a distinguished audience as you are. I am indeed humbled and sincerely grateful for this opportunity to reflect into my past, and to answer your pertinent questions relevant to the Holocaust Legacy."

The seminar lasted two days. I was impressed by the keen interest to study and teach the Holocaust as manifested by the participants. I was in awe.

5/20/01—SOUTHMINSTER PRESBYTERIAN CHURCH, BEAVERTON, OREGON

Al, an elder in the Southminster Presbyterian Church in Beaverton read the Oregonian newspaper of 4/12/2001, "Shadow of the Holocaust," an article briefly describing my life story. Al invited me to make a presentation at his church. In the early morning, I participated in a discussion group, "Ponder this" and later I attended the services in the sanctuary. The pastor, Ben, let me give the sermon instead of him. This was indeed a great honor. I felt humbled, and frankly, quite jittery, due to the fact that it was the first time that I had shared my story with a church audience. I was very grateful when my presentation, "Reflection on the Holocaust," was warmly received. I was moved to tears when I heard the choir's hymn, "The God of Abraham Praise."

Before leaving the sanctuary for the reception, each and every congregant approached me with a stretched-out hand, or put an arm around me. A young lady asked me, "May I hug you?"

"Sure, go ahead. I come from New York. Over there they mugged me, without permission!" I said.

About a year later, one of the church members recognized me at the Beaverton Farmer's market, and stopped me.

"Mr. Wiener, my son and I heard your sermon last year. Since then my son is not the same. He never cared to sit and eat with us. Having heard about your cherished values, and the pains of starvation, our son tries now to find the time to eat with us at the table, and appreciates everything on the table, which is something he never did before."

I was gratified that my message had indeed positively impacted that young man.

I became friendly with Al and I have returned to his church several times since.

6/13/01—CEDAR PARK MIDDLE SCHOOL, PORTLAND, OREGON

Entering the auditorium of Cedar Park Middle School, I was surprised to see students sitting on the floor. This was the last day of school, a joyful day of the school year. However, I was honored to deliver the commencement speech to 175 eighth graders. Chris F., the teacher who invited me, felt that my solemn theme of the Holocaust befitted the students to sit on the floor, to discomfort them, to breathe in a taste of the atmosphere that I came from. Despite their uncomfortable position, the students behaved very respectfully. They listened attentively and asked relevant questions.

Later on, due to a shortened time schedule, the students were allotted only fifteen minutes to write their responses to my presentation. I was very impressed reading the 160 letters they mailed me. I am reproducing below, by their written permission, one letter from a teacher and the other from a student.

What an honor to hear your story. Your courage, your strength. You speak for millions, their voices are not stilled — we hear them through you.

Every heart who hears you keeps their memories alive. Their spirit lives on.

Thank you. Thank you. I will never forget, the students who heard will never forget.

Thank you for the once in a lifetime priviledge of hearing you speak.

Shalom.

Robin Rose

Dear Mr. Wiener,

 I can not express through words how privileged I was to hear your story Wednesday. You reached deep into my heart & I admire all you have done in your life. There is no way I can thank you enough for your words, they are engraved on my soul & I will cherish the things you shared forever. You are a symbol of love, faith, & tolerance that I will strive to come close to my entire life. Your positive attitude even after all you have been through amazes me. I am refreshed by your message of love over hate and I was truely blessed to learn from you. Thankyou very much.

Sincerely, Lauren King

6/4/01—FIREHOUSE CULTURAL CENTER, PORTLAND, OREGON

In March 2001, Alexa D., and her friend Danielle came to interview me for a play, entitled, "Stories from the Holocaust" to be performed by students from a college performing art class. The interview lasted several hours.

Two months later, these two girls with another eight students, performed at the above location, the aforementioned play, based on my Holocaust experience, and several other survivors' stories. The show went on for several weeks before full houses, and was applauded by the audiences and the press.

I told the student who played the role of my tribulations upon arrival in concentration camp, Waldenburgh, that he will probably remember my number 64735, for many years after my passing. He was moved.

9/25/01—WARNER PACIFIC COLLEGE, PORTLAND, OREGON

A small Christian liberal arts college invited me to share my life story with about 300 students of different ages, and faculty members. The audience warmly welcomed me and later the president of the college, Dr. Barber, invited me to have lunch with several professors, who presented me with many questions pertaining to faith, philosophy, education, and political and personal matters. I was flattered to spend hours with such distinguished faculty members.

One day, I stepped into a bookstore and the cashier who recognized me, said, "You are Mr. Wiener who spoke at Warner Pacific College. Your message about the importance of education and the power of love is well etched in my memory."

I was obviously flattered to be recognized by someone in the crowd who had met me a year earlier. I expressed my appreciation for his compliment. As for love, I quoted, "Love is the ultimate and the highest goal to which man can aspire. The salvation of man is through love and in love."

10/5/01—SOUTH SALEM HIGH SCHOOL, SALEM, OREGON

This is the second time that I have been invited by the same teacher to the above school. Her letter touched me deeply.

Al—

The first time I heard you speak, I was overwhelmed with emotion. I felt a need to personally apologize and extend my sorrow to you for all you had been through. The second time I heard you speak, it was to my students. I was in awe of you as a teacher. You were able to help my students find hope out of all the atrocities that had occurred in the Holocaust and those that continue in the world today. This last time that I heard you speak, I was not blinded by sorrow or awe for you. This time I personally connected to your message. You said that we should honor our mother and father because they had lived longer and had learned more from their experiences. We would be lucky, you said, if we could learn from our parents wisdom rather than having to experience events first hand. I am lucky to have met you Al. Even though you are not my father, I have learned to treasure life as it is. I have learned to truly release all hate from my thoughts about groups of people. And I have learned how to teach others. You have strengthened these traits in me. You. Because of your willingness to share your life and the man that you have become, I am lucky.

With Love & Respect—

Jennifer Harris-Clippinger

10/14/01—ST ANTHONY'S CATHOLIC
CHURCH, FOREST GROVE, OREGON

I was warmly received by that audience of about 200 students and parents, all members of the church.

I mentioned that in the concentration camp, Waldneburg, I was stripped of everything personal; my clothing was replaced by a prisoner's uniform without pockets and my name Alter Wiener was replaced by a prisoner's number **64735**. Towards the end of my presentation, a young congregant stood up and loudly addressed me.

"Please give us your number again; all of us will remember your number until the end of our days."

11/03/01—CHRISTIAN LIFE CENTER, ALOHA, OREGON

Fine Arts Pastor at the Christian Life Center in Aloha, Oregon asked me to address the cast of "The Hiding Place." I watched the play. It was the true story of Corrie ten Boom who, along with her family, harbored Jews and Dutch resisters in their home during World War II. Betrayed to the Germans, Corrie ten Boom, her father, and sister were imprisoned in Nazi concentration camps where all perished, except for Corrie. She spent the remainder of her life traveling throughout sixty countries where, as a writer and inspirational speaker, she promoted Christian values. For her work as a rescuer, she was honored in Israel as a "Righteous Gentile" at *Yad Vashem* (Holocaust Memorial Museum).

After the performance, the cast of about fifty performers listened at rapt attention to my story, trying to find the inextricable link in my true story to the true story that they had just portrayed in the play.

12/15/01—WARNER PACIFIC COLLEGE,
PORTLAND, OREGON

I shared my story with about 300 students on September 25, 2001. Three months later, Warner Pacific College presented me with an honorary bachelor's degree, during its winter commencement. This was the only time in its sixteen-year history that Warner awarded an honorary degree to anybody. I was obviously very humbled by that honor.

I was moved to tears when the audience of about 400 students, guests and distinguished faculty members, gave me a standing ovation. The event was aired on the evening's news and received write-ups in several newspapers. I had a feeling of disbelief. Below is one picture of the event and one pertinent article. It had indeed been a very eventful day for me.

I thanked Professor Jay Barber, the president of the college, for the award and I said, "While being incarcerated in concentration camps, I had two dreams; one to be reunited with my family, which tragically did not materialize. I am the only survivor of my immediate family. The other dream was to be able to eat as much bread as I wanted, to sleep on a mattress, to be able to walk freely, to worship at liberty, to associate at will, and to regain my human rights. Thank God, this dream did materialize in this blessed country of the U.S.A. However, I have never dreamt that one day such a distinguished audience as you shall honor me. Many of you professors enjoy prestige. As a graduate of just five classes of elementary school, I have no impressive academic credentials to show. I am extremely humbled to be your guest today. I am very grateful to those of you graduates, who were raptly listening to my presentation three months ago. I would just like to repeat several phrases stemming from my empirical life. I have learned that

Survivor Al Wiener gets honorary degree

Hillsboro resident and Holocaust survivor Al Wiener was awarded an honorary bachelor's degree from Warner Pacific College at commencement ceremonies Dec. 15

Wiener, 75, is a member of the Oregon Holocaust Resource Center's Speaker Bureau. He spends much of his time sharing his story with audiences at schools, churches and elsewhere.

"It is Al Wiener's special way of speaking and teaching that has prompted Warner Pacific College to bestow an honorary degree upon him," said WPC official Scott Thompson.

AL WIENER

"Mr. Wiener humbly stands before his audiences and encourages them to cherish the education he never had the opportunity to receive. It is his message of tolerance and love entwined with his life story that makes him so deserving of the award."

Wiener was born in Poland and was 13 years old when the German army invaded his hometown of Chizanow in September 1939. His formal education ended at that age, and at age 15 he was deported to a Nazi labor camp, the first of five different camps in which he was incarcerated over three years.

At his liberation in May 1945, Wiener was so emaciated that the doctors gave him no hope for survival.

But Wiener did survive, the only one of more than 100 members of his extended family.

ignorance is the enemy of mankind. The real property of man is not what he owns but what he knows. Whatever you put in your head, no one can take it away from you. It is the fountain of knowledge that will enrich your life, and not excesses of consumerism. Hate hatred and remove the term from your vocabulary. Love, for your fellow man, not just romantic love, will contribute to a happy life. Sanction the sanctity of life and enjoy it."

This acknowledgment and the warm reception overwhelmed me.

1/25/02—NATIONAL ASSOC. OF INSURANCE AND FINANCIAL ADVISORS, BEAVERTON, OREGON

I shared my Holocaust experience with about 300 insurance agents and financial advisors at a convention that took place at the Greenwood Inn.

After my presentation, a man (and his wife) approached me and asked my forgiveness for the suffering brought upon me by the Nazis. I said to him," Looking at you, I know you could not have been involved in the war because you are so young."

The man said, "It is not me, but my father who was a Nazi, and I have been living with a guilty feeling all my life."

I responded, "Sir, there is nothing for me to forgive you. You did not participate in the genocide. You are not responsible for your father's action or inaction."

We shook hands and the man was pleased that I did not hate him.

As is commonly practiced at conventions, small souvenirs, or mementos, such as keychains, pens, etc., are given out to the participants. I was presented with a small blanket. I thanked the audience and said," When King David was old and frail, his lieutenants brought him a young maid and you expect me to settle for a blanket?! I expected you advisors to be more sophisticated than the advisors in Biblical times."

3/15/02—WOODBURN HIGH SCHOOL, WOODBURN, OREGON

The teacher, Wendi K., was very gracious and most of the 300 ninth graders behaved respectfully. I was stunned hearing one student's question, "Were there any Mexicans in the concentration camps?"

The teacher was somewhat embarrassed and for me it was indicative of how little some students know about history and how important it is for me to share my Holocaust experience with them.

4/6/02—COMMUNITY ARTS CENTER, ASTORIA, OREGON

I was welcomed by Carol N., and Katherine M. They accommodated me in a private home owned by Finish immigrants (like many of Astoria's residents). In the afternoon, I spoke to an audience of about 220 students, and in the evening to about 100 people of the community.

Taking a stroll in this quaint town, I noticed that my photo (the one taken shortly after my liberation from concentration camp) was in the windows of many stores.

I stepped into a bookstore and while paying for a book that I had bought, I told the cashier, "I am the man whose photo is in your store window."

Bursting into tears, she embraced me and told me that many of her distant relatives perished during the Holocaust.

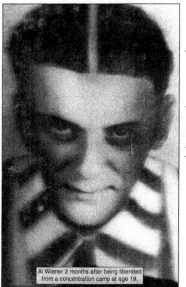

Al Wiener 2 months after being liberated from a concentration camp at age 19.

Hosted by Carol Newman
Friday, April 5th • 1:00 PM & 7:30 PM
CCC Performing Art Center • 16th & Franklin, Astoria

HOLOCAUST REMEMBRANCE

Featuring two speakers, Ruth Bolliger and Al Wiener from the Oregon Holocaust Resource Center in Forest Grove, Oregon. Both are survivors of the Holocaust.

The afternoon presentation at 1:00 PM is free.
The evening presentation at 7:30 PM is a ticketed event.

Tickets: $8 General, $6 Student/Senior, $3 Children under 12
Tickets can be purchased at the Clatsop Community College Library; at the CCC South County Center in Seaside and at Old Town Framing, Astoria; and by phone at 338-2473. The box office at the Performing Arts Center opens one hour prior to the event.
Proceeds benefit the Oregon Holocaust Resource Center.

Ruth Bolliger

⊕ARTS & IDEAS

Presented by Clatsop Community College Arts & Ideas Series • (503) 338-2473 • www.clatsopcc.edu/arts&ideas

4/8/02 TO 5/502—ANNE FRANK INTERNATIONAL EXHIBIT, PORTLAND, OREGON

The exhibit, sponsored by several organizations, including OHRC took place at Lloyd Center Shopping Mall. It was very well attended, especially by students who were bussed in from schools across the state of Oregon and South Washington.

As a Holocaust survivor, I was asked to share my story with the visitors at the exhibit. I spoke at three sessions, on each of the five assigned days. The picture below is from one of those sessions.

4/10/02—LEWIS AND CLARK COLLEGE, PORTLAND, OREGON

Professor Mathew L. was referred to me by another professor from Pacific University. I received a letter from each of the forty-five students in the class. The one below is from a student inspired to be a better person.

April, 2002

Mr. Wiener,

I'm not entirely sure what to say to you. I was very much looking forward to hearing you speak, being in the presence of someone who had experienced a life so dramatically different from my own, all at my age. I am nineteen, and I can't even imagine living through what you did. And yet, your talk was nothing shocking or new to me; I have seen + heard it before. What caught me + really made me appreciate what you had to say was seeing you. The vibrance and true passion for life that you exude, even with all of the adversity that came your way. And it is for this that I wish to say thank you. Thank you for continuing to love life and what it has to offer. Thank you for your unconditional faith in the character of mankind. For being the amazing spirit that you are, I express my gratitude. It is all the more inspirational to hear about forgiveness from a person with your past. I vow to learn all I can in the growing educational experience I am priveleged enough to have. My grandfather was schooled only through 5th grade, and I feel for his thirst for knowledge that was left so unquenched. I vow to look for the good in people, + forgive those who have done me wrong. Thank you for inspiring me to be a better person.

5/23/02—PIONEER HERITAGE ACADEMY, BEAVERTON, OREGON

I shared my life story with forty students, of different ages, in this Mormon school.

All the students wrote letters and put them into one large envelope addressed to, "To the Amazing Mr. Wiener" (rather than my first name).

The mail carrier said to me, "I have seen all kind of odd addressed envelopes, but never had such an addressed envelope. What is so amazing about you?"

"The mere fact that I am here and alive!" was my terse answer.

9/13/02—W.P. LORD HIGH SCHOOL, WOODBURN, OREGON

This facility is for young boys who violated the law. They serve different terms while being enabled to pursue their studies (middle school and high school).

When I opened my presentation with, "I am coming from hell," one of the inmates shouted back, "We are here in hell, too."

My response was, "You are not in hell; you are in a Hilton Hotel."

I meant it! There is absolutely no comparison.

"I have noticed the beautiful landscape, the private cells, the medical care, the adequate feeding, the opportunity to learn, the ability to communicate with the outside world by phone and mail, the occasion for family visits, the absence of personal abuse, such as indiscriminate beatings, the limited time of incarceration, and no fear to be annihilated. I had none of those rights and benefits when I was incarcerated in forced labor and concentration camps. I faced starvation and annihilation. Furthermore, I had committed no offenses."

One inmate asked me if in forced labor camps I had ever been "high." I responded, "We had no access to any licit or illicit drugs. Also, when you are starving you are not craving to be "high" (euphoric or intoxicated).

All your thoughts and impulses focus on how to get a piece of bread or a potato, or to quench your thirst.

I was quite apprehensive and frankly not enthusiastic "to go to jail" but when I had noticed that most of the 100 young offenders were attentive and respectful, I felt gratified. When I saw tears from some faces, I realized that I had stirred some dormant emotions. This was indeed an opportunity to make a change for the better in those young mens' lives, as I was told by the school/prison's instructors.

11/06/02—MILWAUKIE HIGH SCHOOL, MILWAUKIE, OREGON

I shared my life story with 1,400 people. The event, titled, "Living History Day" had been designated as a day of honoring the U.S. veterans of World War I, World War II, Korea, Vietnam, and Persian Gulf by the entire students' body of that school. Mr. Ken Buckles, a son of a veteran in the Korean War, introduced the idea for veterans to share their stories with students and for students to give something back to the men and women who have served our country. Mr. Buckles considers Holocaust survivors as veterans, and ergo he invited me to share my story.

11/7/02—CLACKAMAS HIGH SCHOOL, CLACKAMAS, OREGON

I shared my life story with 1,800 people, 1,600 students and about 200 U.S. veterans; the largest audience I have ever spoken to, so far. At the conclusion, about thirty students came to the podium, raised their right hands and proclaimed, "We promise you to stay in school; and never to drop out!" I felt rewarded for my effort to stress the importance of education.

12/8/02—SOUTH PARK UNITARIAN FELLOWSHIP, WEST LINN, OREGON

After my speech, one lady rushed home to bring me two loaves of bread that she had baked the previous day. I was obviously very grateful for that thoughtful symbolic gesture, and I embraced her saying, "Why didn't you bring me this in 1945 when I was starving?"

Her response was, "I wish I could, but I was only eight years old then."

One member introduced himself to me, saying, "I was an officer in the American Army that liberated one of the concentration camps. I no longer remember the name of that camp, but I still have nightmares from the grisly conditions we found in that camp. You must write down your Holocaust experience for the future generations. It is imperative that they learn and appreciate this blessed country of the U.S.A. and do everything in their power to prevent such horrific events from recurring."

1/17/03—OREGON STATE PENITENTIARY, SALEM, OREGON

I shared my life story with 130 inmates of that prison, who belonged to a club of Vietnam War Veterans. I was impressed with the modern facility that the prisoners enjoyed. They are receiving nutritional food, medical care, and many amenities. They have contact with the outside world, by mail, telephone, or visitors. Special privileges are granted for good behavior.

During my incarceration in Nazi concentration camps, none of such social amenities were provided. I obviously committed no offense to justify imprisonment, other than being condemned for belonging to an "inferior race, tainted blood" by Nazi's criteria.

Although those prisoners who listened to my presentation were hard core criminals, I was glad to see them treated humanely. It had been a pleasant surprise to observe the keen interest and respectful attitude most of the prisoners manifested during, and at the conclusion of, my presentation. I was gratified when several prisoners expressed their bewilderment and admiration for my message of tolerance and those values instilled in me by my family's environment in Poland.

At the conclusion of my presentation, one prisoner had said to me, "If I had heard thirty years ago about your suffering experienced during the Holocaust, I would have appreciated what I had and not done—something foolish that brought me in here."

1/21/03—PACIFIC UNIVERSITY, FOREST GROVE, OREGON

I shared my life story with about 100 students whose instructor was Mike S., a well-versed professor in the history of the Holocaust. He has been very active in perpetuating the Holocaust legacy. Mike had heard my story, on several other occasions, and wrote an article, on November 20, 2002, published in the News-Times, about the importance of education as expressed in my presentations.

One student approached me later on and said to me, "I had a friend whom I hated, because of a fall-out, but listening to you talk about tolerance, I shall call him tonight and make amends."

Below is another student's letter pertaining to hate. She loved my hug!

Dear Mr. Wiener,   February 10, 2003

I wanted to thank you for coming to our class and sharing your story. I am sure you have heard this before, but reading and learning about the Holocaust did not mean nearly as much to me until I heard you speak. You have a very powerful message and I feel blessed to have heard it. To tell you the truth, I was expecting you to be bitter and even vengeful toward those who had caused you pain and suffering. However, you were not bitter at all and it is because you are a very loving person that you are able to forgive. I have been told many times in my life that remaining angry about something does not solve anything. Although I have known this, I did not completely understand what it meant to forgive someone. There is no room for hate when I love and am

loved by others. Love is the only thing that matters. I figured that if you were able to forgive those who had caused you and your family to suffer, that I had no right holding grudges against those who have hurt me. Especially since I have never lived through and experienced anything as horrific as the Holocaust. I have a loving family, great friends, and a wonderful life. Your strength and your story made me realize how important that all is to me and I am grateful. I am sure it is not easy for you to speak of the Holocaust but I am glad that you did and it made a big impression on all of us. This card is a painting of City Hall in my hometown Baker City, Oregon. It is a beautiful town and I wanted to share it with you, as you have shared your story with me.

P.S. you give great hugs too!

2/19/03—OASIS C/O MEIER & FRANK, PORTLAND, OREGON

I spoke to a group of fifty senior citizens, who are members of this organization. My presentation, which lasted two hours, was very well received by the mature audience that included people who remembered World War II. One woman told me that she was familiar with the camps that I had mentioned in my speech, because she was born in that region.

3/11/03—PENDLETON HIGH SCHOOL, PENDLETON, OREGON

I traveled (a four-hour drive) on a charted bus that took me, with fifty other war veterans, to Pendleton High School for "Living History Day." The following day I spoke to the entire student body (950 students) plus about 100 war veterans. All students were formally dressed and had no regular classes.

I was humbled to be the key speaker at the event, and very moved by the attentive audience and the spontaneous standing ovation. In the afternoon, the school principal, and the students' president recognized the contribution made by the several speakers to the success of the event. At 2:00 p.m., on the way out to the parking lot, I walked between two columns of about 400 students on each side, who applauded, embraced me, and thanked me for being their guest.

3/23/03—THE ZION LUTHERAN CHURCH, CAMAS, WASHINGTON

I shared my Holocaust experience with 300 congregants. I had never dreamt in my entire life that a day would come when I would be warmly embraced by a congregation.

The Nazis' regime deemed me to be a defective trait; the respect and honor that the congregation bestowed upon me was just a wonderful antidote to that characterization.

The singing of Shalom, partially in Hebrew, by the church choir was a profound gesture. It moved me to tears. The spontaneous standing ovation chased away the residue of the terrible episodes I had been dwelling on in my presentations. I was invited to stand with the pastor, at the exit door to shake hands with each congregant. None of them had ever met a Holocaust survivor. It had indeed been an eventful day for me that I shall never forget.

4/18/04—GESHER CONGREGATION, PORTLAND, OREGON

I spoke to about sixty adults and children participating in Passover Seder. Below are my comments at the festive occasion:

> *Dear Rabbi Laurie, Rabbi Gary and guests,*
>
> *Thanks for inviting me and for granting me an opportunity, during the Haggadah reading, to share a glimpse of my enslavement experience during the Holocaust, with your guests at the Seder, a gracious gesture indeed.*
>
> *For me, as a Holocaust survivor, it was indeed an eventful evening, and a learning experience. I can assure you that while being incarcerated in concentration camps, I could not have imagined that one day I would be able to recite the Biblical story of the Exodus, and simultaneously have the freedom to relay my horrific Holocaust experience to a diverse audience, in a caravan occupied by celebrating Jews and non-Jews, smiling children, loaded food trays, and two distinguished Rabbis.*

5/17/03—SW WA SYNOD EVANGELICAL LUTHERAN CHURCH, TACOMA, WASHINGTON

Several hundred clergy and lay people attended the above convention. "Holocaust Lessons" was one out of seven workshops scheduled in the convention's program.

I was humbled to share my life story with a distinguished group of the faithful and to have an impact on those who heard me, as reflected below in a pastor's letter:

5-19-03

dear Alter,

Again, our heart-felt thanks for enriching the lives of the ELCA Lutherans at the SW Synod Convention on Sat., May 17th. What an honor to hear you and the audience left with your message of, "hate hatred" and your deeply-embedded values that stood up against nazi brutality. Out of the hell of the camps, you emerged as a witness and articulate gift to the world to embrace diversity and to be ever vigilent. Evil is never far from emerging its ugly head throughout our world.

Scrabble & dinner -- June, 2003!
* I add my thanks and appreciation ⟨Hannelore⟩ for all your efforts to get to the Doubletree and to persevere with no microphone. You are always so full of grace & resiliency. Tom

154

5/18/03—IN DEFENSE OF ANIMALS, PORTLAND, OREGON

I shared my Holocaust and vegetarianism experiences with a group of animal lovers. The audience was very respectful and attentive to my presentation. However, I disagreed with the frequent usage of the term Holocaust in their publications pertinent to the U.S. culture of killing animals for consumption. I found Holocaust references particularly odious, especially when capitalized.

5/19/03—MORRISON CENTER, PORTLAND, OREGON

A small group of young men who have been adjudicated for sexually abusive behavior listened raptly to my life story. After my presentation, one fourteen-year-old inmate/student told me, "I have just realized how good of a life I had, and still have it even here, in comparison to what you went through, at my age. God bless you."

I couldn't have agreed more!

7/13/03—WASHINGTON COUNTY SHERIFF'S OFFICE, HILLSBORO, OREGON

Most of the seventy inmates were quite respectful and listened to my story. However, one inmate told me bluntly, "I do not believe that there were ovens in Auschwitz and that Germans burned innocent people. It is just an improvised complex put up by the Polish government to make it a tourist attraction."

It was shocking and very painful to me to hear such an outrageous distortion. I started to reason with the man, but a jail guard pulled me away, saying, "This man is a Skin-Head, and you cannot reason with him. He is here for a racial assault. I am sorry for this unpleasant encounter."

3/5/04—ST HELEN HIGH SCHOOL, ST HELENS, OREGON

Out of forty-seven letters, I share below one from a teacher that encompasses all aspects of the Holocaust Legacy:

Dear Mr. Wiener,

I am writing to thank you from the bottom of my heart for coming to speak to my students. Not only was it a fabulous learning experience for them but it also was a deeply moving experience for me. There are not words that can accurately express what I experienced as I listened to you, but I will try to explain as best I can.

I find it incredible that despite all of the horror you experienced in your early life, you never questioned your faith. In a life that was so filled with pain and suffering, I don't think I would have had the strength to continue to believe like you did. One thing you said has resonated with me since you spoke here and that was about the man who prayed every day and said, when asked how he could still pray with all that was happening, that he was thankful that he was not like the Nazis. That really struck a chord with me. I keep thinking about that comment and thanking God that I too am not a person who is cruel like that.

We, as a society, so rarely give thanks for the things that are really important in life and I am guilty of this. I forget that things like a roof over my head and food and freedom and the love of my family are the most important things I have. I think you helped all of these students realize, even if just for an hour or two, that they have a lot to be thankful for. They may not remember everything you said that day, but they will remember that they once met an amazing man who survived the Holocaust and came to tell them about it.

You are a brave, sweet, wonderful person and I feel it is an honor to have met you. I do believe that "ignorance is the enemy of mankind" and education is the way to make sure that events like the Holocaust never happen again. I am committed to doing everything I can to help my students understand that. But my students are not the main reason I do this. The main reason I am constantly teaching and learning and trying to improve the world is so that my daughter, and the other children Nathan and I hope to have someday, will have a better world to live in. Tacy just turned one in February; she is the most important person in my life and the most perfect thing I have ever done. I love her more than anything and I want to make sure that the things that you went through never happen to her or any child. I know that when she is old enough, I will share your life story and message with her. You are helping to change the world one person at a time and I think everyone can learn from your persistence, faith, strength, love, and utter belief in the goodness of mankind.

Thank you, Mr. Wiener, for changing my life and for helping me better understand the Holocaust and the world I live in. I will always remember you in my heart and I hope that I will have the opportunity to meet you again. Please keep talking about your experiences and sharing the story of your life for as long as you can. The good you do is immeasurable and the lives you have changed are countless.

With deepest respect and humble appreciation,

Carrie McCallum

Carrie McCallum

3/10/04—PENDLETON HIGH SCHOOL, PENDLETON, OREGON

There were 1,000 people in the audience. Below are expressive faces of some students.

Al Wiener, Holocaust survivor, talks to students after giving a presentation to the entire Pendleton High School student body during Living History Day.

Photo by Dan Cresswell of the East Oregonian

3/18/04—PATTON MIDDLE SCHOOL, MCMINNVILLE. OREGON

Seventy eighth graders listened attentively to my life story. One student told me, "I am a very vengeful person, but will be no more as of tomorrow thanks to you, Mr. Wiener."

I was gratified to hear that, and even more so when one student wrote that I saved her life.

Dear Alter Wiener,

I want to thank you for coming to talk at my school. You made me realize that I still had so much to live for and that life is precious. Your story made me really think about what I have and others don't. the freedom I have that I take for granted. I always thought my life was unfair and I was living a hell. To some extent it was, but you lived through something I wouldn't dream of. By telling us your story you saved my life. I had planned on killing myself the next day. I'm glad you did. My Grandma wanted me to thank you, I also told her pieces of your story and she was moved. thank you so much for teaching me that life is something to treasure.

Sincerely,

3/19/04—A STUDENT FROM GERMANY

Niqui, an exchange student from Köln Germany, interviewed me for several hours.

Her grandfather was in the German Army, and Niqui has been living with a guilt-feeling that her grandfather might have been involved in committing atrocities during the Holocaust. I assured Niqui that I have no hatred in my heart against the German people and definitely no bad feelings against the new generations of the German people. Niqui and I became friends, and I am willing to shake a friendly hand with any German who has not been involved in mass killing of innocent people, Jews or others.

4/5/04—JACKSON MIDDLE SCHOOL, PORTLAND, OREGON

I was moved by reading the seventy-two students' letters from the above school. The letter below, from a student whose mother passed away, was very poignant.

Dear Mr. Wiener,
Thank you so very much for sharing your amazing story with us. I can't believe all the pain you went through. My Mother recently passed away from ovarian cancer, I remember going to see her a hour after she had died. The look on her face I'll never forget. It was so hard for me, seeing her, but she wasn't there. I thought the pain I endured was tremendous, but after hearing how you stared your father, decomposing, right in the face... and how you survived so much torture, the agony. Your talk today really showed me how fortunate I am to have my Dad, my Grandma, my family. Your talk was very insperational, and I will never forget. Thanks again. 64735.

4/22/04—REDMOND HIGH SCHOOL, REDMOND, OREGON

The audience of over 2,000 people consisted of the entire school body, U.S. war veterans, and members from the Redmond community. This was the largest group I shared my life story with; and I received hundreds of letters. Below are two of them. One was from a student who changed his mind from moving out and will stay with his family. Another was from a student who will be more appreciative.

Dear Mr. Wiener,

Thank you for sharing you story with me. When you told us that you had to pick out your father, it made me think about my dad. Just before you came I was moving my stuff out and giving up on my family. When you told us your story it made me think about how hard he tryes to please me. You alone kept my family in my life.

Thank you.

April 23, 2004

ALTER WIENER
7065 NE. RONIER WAY, APT 1216
HILLSBORO, OR 97124 - 7922

Dear Mr. Wiener,

I just wanted to tell you how much I truly appreciated your presentation for our school yesterday. I cannot convey to you how much it really meant to me. I have grown up with every imenity available and have never had enough appreciation for it all. That is, until yesterday. You gave me a whole new appreciation for everything I have and all the freedoms I am allowed. Your stories deeply moved me, mainly because of what happened to your family. I love my family very much, and imagining the loss of them was very hard. I have great empathy for you and all others involved in such a tragedy. Also, I have heard much about this time in history, but never truly understood or comrehended the huge effects it had on those involved. Now I see it. It is the worst thing imaginable and you were able to endure through it all. You give me the faith and courage to get through life and any trials that come my way. I will not forget you and I am sure that no one else will either. Thank you for the loving kindness you showwed in coming to see us. Remain strong and couragous always.

Love and Friendship,

I was surprised how the eleven-year-old students were attentive to my presentation. I was touched by the teacher's letter, below:

Dear Mr. Wiener,

Thank you dearly for coming to our class and sharing your story. You are an inspiration to us all. You have taught the students such an invaluable lesson – the importance of love, appreciation, and education. Thank you for making us all stop and appreciate all that we have. Thank you for teaching us true courage and the power of strength and values. And last but not least, thank you for modeling love and compassion instead of hate and anger.

We live in an age where war, fighting, name-calling, stealing, and cheating is modeled frequently in the media and in war. You have shown us that we can be better than that. In all situations, we need to pull from our inner strength and practice problem solving, patience, and compassion.

Thank you for being our hero!

Gratefully,
Nicole Rocklag

5/5/05—SOUTH METRO JEWISH CONGREGATION, WEST LINN, OREGON

I was allotted twenty minutes to share my life story with an audience of Jews, Christians and intermarried couples. The occasion was *Yom-Hashoa*, a Holocaust memorial service.

After my presentation, a young lady approached me saying, "I know Chrzanów the town you are coming from, since my grandmother was born there."

It turned out that that lady and I had the same great-grandfather; I found a second cousin.

10/22/05—WASHINGTON STATE HOLOCAUST EDUCATION CENTER, SEATTLE, WASHINGTON

I shared my life story with thirty teachers:

5/5/06—LOWER COLUMBIA COLLEGE, LONGVIEW, WASHINGTON

The beautiful and generous teacher gave me a stone from the Berlin Wall. She had chipped it by herself while visiting Germany at that time when the Wall was turned down.

I cherish that historical memento. I pray that all mental walls that separate peoples will be demolished and replaced by malls that bring them together.

Two students' appreciation for my presentation appear below.

Dear Al, This is a card a student wrote to me about you! Love, Terrie

Thank you again for inviting Mr. Wiener to be a guest speaker for our class. It was an incredible experience for me. It brought tears to my eyes to listen to him recounting his horrific experiences. It made me appreciate the life that I live. If I learn nothing from this class, it will have been worth it just for hearing him speak. It was the highlight of my college career so far.

When I got home that afternoon, I recounted Mr. Wieners' story to my wife. It brought tears to her eyes as well. I looked at my 5-year old son and thanked God that he will never have to experience the things that Mr. Wiener lived through.

On November 22nd, 2005, my cousin and best friend of 25 years killed himself by jumping off the top of a building. I believe that if my

Over →

Friend had heard Mr. Wiener's speech, that he might have realized just how temporary and trivial his problems really were, and not jumped.

Mr. Wiener is a living part of history I am glad that you gave me the opportunity to hear his story and shake his hand. By the time most of the kids in this class reach our age (I am 37 yrs. old) the opportunity to hear testimony from an actual holocaust survivor in person will be gone. I hope that all of them saw the privilege in what they were allowed to attend on Friday. I hope that they all appreciated it as much as I did.

Sincerely,

October 8, 2006

Dear Mr. Wiener,

I would like to thank you for your time and for sharing your experiences. I try to imagine the terrible things you went through. I know I will never know your pain and sorrow. To be taken away and have your whole life and security stripped away one piece at a time until you stand alone in the cold. It is amazing that you could go through so much and be so compassionate and non-judgmental. You're a incredibly strong man. I can see why God chosen you to tell your stories. You I am sure you have touched more people than you know. You have given so much and had so much taken from you. Mr. Wiener you are a true hero. I thank you for being who you are. This story has helped me to see a lot of things in this world different and surely to count my blessings. I thank the German women that had the courage and compassion to help you. Your story and you have made a deep impression upon my heart. God Bless

MY ANSWERS TO QUESTIONS
FROM THE AUDIENCE

Q: *I have read that some leaders in the U.S. advocated appeasing Hitler. Could you please give some historical background?*

APPEASEMENT

In the 1930s, there was a strong antiwar movement in the U.S. They called themselves the "Appeasers!" Remembering and still mourning the heavy casualties of World War I, the appeasers understandably wanted to avoid another war at all costs. Most Americans failed to see Hitler as a genocidal megalomaniac. The American isolationists' sentiments before Pearl Harbor were very powerful. They closed their conscience and failed to take into consideration that such a great power as their country has also great moral responsibility. The President of Czechoslovakia, Edward Benes, warned the Western Democracies in 1937 that Hitler's ambitions could not be appeased.

On September 29, 1938, England, France, Italy, and Germany signed an agreement demanding that Czechoslovakia capitulate. Benes resigned, and the Germans occupied the Sudetenland. Neville Chamberlain, the British prime minister, declared then that the Munich Agreement would, "….ensure peace in our time." He disastrously tried to reason with Hitler. The League of Nations also lacked concrete policies to commensurate with the threat of Nazism.

The appeasers believed that Hitler should be contained by diplomatic persuasion and perhaps economic sanctions. The appeasers gave Hitler what he wanted. First, they gave him the Rhineland, and then on March 11, 1938 the Nazis crossed the German-Austrian frontier. Finally, they gave him the Sudetenland and the Danzing corridor, but still they could not avert World War II. It just whetted Hitler's appetite and increased his hubris. The appeasers wished to buy time, but Hitler used that time to build up his military strength, which was in violation of the Versailles treaty.

Eventually World War II broke out on September 1, 1939. Six million Jews and five million "undesirables" were murdered. A total of 62 million lives were lost in World War II. Neville Chamberlain and Edouard Daladier announced to the world that a generation of peace was at hand after their return in 1938 from signing the Munich Pact with Hitler. Winston Churchill told Chamberlain, "You were given the choice between war and dishonor. You chose dishonor, and you will have war."

Trying to placate a tyrant who does not hesitate to murder his own people has never worked. Adolph Hitler, Joseph Stalin, Mao, Pol-Pot, and Idi Amin were evil tyrants at heart, power-hungry and opportunists. Tyrants of the 21st century are also incorrigible and not redeemable.

"His mouth is filled with false oaths, with deception and malice. Under his tongue are mischief and iniquity. He waits in ambush near open cities. In hidden places, he numbers the innocent." King David wrote this thousands of years ago, in Psalms 10:7-8.

> *"Man's inhumanity to man is not only perpetrated by the vitriolic actions of those who are bad, it is also perpetrated by the vitiating inaction of those who are good."*
> (Rev. Martin Luther King, Jr.)

> *"The only thing necessary for evil to flourish is for good men to do nothing."*
> (British 18th century philosopher, Edmund Burke)

Q: *I do appreciate the good life I have, but many of my classmates are always grumbling, including those who have it even better than I have. What will make them to be more appreciative?*

APPRECIATION

Many Americans often forget, but I always remember and appreciate our freedom. There is no place in the world that enjoys the sheer openness as we do in the U.S.A.

Hillary Clinton writes in her book, *It Takes a Village*, about a fifteen-year-old girl whom she personally knew, who committed suicide. The girl left a note, saying, "I don't think that I am strong enough to be a teenager in today's world." If the girl would have compared her problems with the ones I had to face at her age, she would have realized the senselessness of her action. Did I have the physical and emotional strength in concentration camps to strive for survival? Was that girl starving as I was? If she would have visited places where freedom is a rare commodity and food is not available or affordable, she might have appreciated her living conditions and not killed herself.

There is always something to be grateful for even under the most difficult circumstances. Do we need a shaking of a natural or manmade disaster to be more appreciative of our blessings? Most people in this country, in our times, take things for granted. They forget that nothing should ever be taken for granted, not even life! Just as you are prone to die at any moment, so may unexpected events carry away those "granted" privileges!

I would suggest to any chronic grumbler, to write down every morning the things that she or he has to be thankful for: I am not hungry; I am not cold; I am not beaten, I have my family; I have my freedom to learn, to associate, and to worship. I am indeed snug and comfy! If you can find one good thing in a bad situation, then negativity will never defeat you. There is so much to be grateful for. We do not have to be grateful only when something wonderful happens. If you observe the blooming of one flower and neglect to appreciate the blooming of the other flowers, you miss the beauty of the entire garden.

I am bewildered and saddened when many children in the U.S. seem to be so discontent. Most kids in this country have everything they want and still they seem to be disturbed. I remember poor kids in my hometown who were always playful and smiling. I never heard of kids committing suicide when I was a kid. Today many kids who have never experienced hardship in their childhood choose to end their life.

> *"The one that rejoices in his portion is rich"*
> (Avoth 4,1)

> *"We should give thanks for everything we have, instead of worrying about what we don't have. To know when you have enough is to be rich beyond measure."*
> (Lau Tzu)

> *"A grateful mind is a great mind; it eventually attracts to itself every great thing."*
> (Plato 427-347)

Q: *You mentioned that the Polish authorities prevented your father from fleeing his home in order to provide the Polish retreating army with goods from his business. What kind of business was it? Also, if the war would not have interrupted your life, would you today be in that business and not in U.S.? My other question is; how could anybody conduct business when there were no telephones? I am so used to a telephone and wonder how I could live without it.*

BUSINESS

In our community in Chrzanów, Poland, when a father was a shoemaker, a tailor, a teacher, a preacher, or a potter, the son's occupation was expected to be in the same line. Very rarely did a son opt for a career other than his father's. It would be considered an invalidation of traditional values. If fate had determined otherwise, I would have probably become part of my father's business, a landmark in our town's landscape for over 100 years. My father and his brothers inherited the business from their father who had inherited it from his father, and so on.

It was a wholesale business of basic foodstuff, imported products, and household wares. Deliveries to the store and warehouses were made mostly by horse-drawn carriages that picked up the goods at the local railroad station. There were no telephones, so all business transactions, such as orders for supplies, were made by snail mail. If urgent communication was needed, a frachter, an errand, by walking or a messenger by bike, or by train, picked up the envelope or package to deliver. It was similar to FedEx nowadays, but it was obviously much slower. Workers carried sacks of flower, sugar, rice, etc. on their shoulders and either stacked them or delivered them to the retailers. There were no forklifts.

I used to marvel at my father's arithmetic. There were no calculators in those days, and all multiplications and addition had to be figured out in one's head. Invoices were handwritten. Contracts were seldom used, and a handshake sufficed.

I do recall once asking my father, "Why does a Suchard chocolate bar cost so much and a Wendel bar cost more?"

He told me, "All items in this store are priced according to their estimated value by the buyers at the time of the sale."

I hardly understood his explanation then, but I do today. The shelves loaded with sweets, delicacies, bins of nuts and grains fascinated me. I wanted to get involved in the vivacious activity. I dreamt that one day I would be able to eat as much chocolate as I wanted.

My father's economic status was not always in my favor. I was often bullied by peers who called me names such as girly, because I was too good-looking for a boy. I had no money to bribe my harassers, because in those days little kids received no weekly allowances. The only time when I did receive some small change, never a bill, was on Hanukkah, The Festival of Lights. So, to pacify my bullies, I bribed them with figs, dates, nuts and candies from my father's store. I became a shoplifter at a very young age. When caught, I was reprimanded. I was embarrassed to reveal that my shoplifting was for ransom.

When World War II broke out, the Polish Zloty lost its nominal value. I remember when bartering became a substitute for paper currency. A great variety of objects such as jewelry, cloths, commodities, and a wide range of valuables had served as money in the adult world, and stones, shells, and beads were popular amongst the children.

War brought a halt to business activities and created disruption to people's livelihood. Rampant destruction of life and property compelled people to suppress their aspirations and divert their energy to improvise means for survival. You could no longer do what you had been trained to do or loved to do. You did what the German authorities forced you to do. Businessmen and professionals, tailors and shoemakers, students and scholars all became slave laborers.

Q: *Did Winston Churchill better understand the menace of Nazism, than Franklin Roosevelt?*

CHURCHILL

Absolutely, Winston Churchill did understand the menace of Nazism. He believed that war is sometimes unavoidable and he would not accept anything less than victory over fascism—the forces of evil.

In May 1940, Churchill confronted a cabinet revolt led by Lord Halifax, who wanted him to get out of the war and make a deal with Hitler in the wake of the Dunkirk debacle and the crumbling of the French and Belgian armies.

Churchill told the British people, "I have nothing to offer but blood, toil, tears and sweat!"

History proved him to be right in his determination to defeat Germany despite the opposition of many and the limited resources at his command. To quote Shakespeare, "Some are born great, some achieve greatness, and some have greatness thrust upon them."

All may be attributed to Churchill.

Q: *The Germans were known to be very cultured. There were many notable artists, and scientists among them. How could so many educated people get involved in committing atrocities?*

CONSCIENCE

Educational credentials did not moderate the Nazis' brutality. Nazis did not have a shred of conscience. Eight out of the sixteen signatories of the "Final Solution" document had Ph.D's. Joseph Goebbels, Hitler's propaganda minister, had three Ph.D's.

The perpetrators of the Holocaust had been well-schooled, and modern. They all had outward traits of cultured men, except for a conscience. Their crimes showed the world that evil can slip in, and blend in, even amid the most civilized surroundings. Only one's conscience can stop it.

The Nazis had no qualms of conscience to burn millions of the innocent. The bones of many victims were chopped and mulched for compost; skins were used for lampshades, and the ashes were used as fertilizers.

Students, when they graduated from medical schools, took the Hippocratic Oath, which one phrase states, "Into whatever house I enter, I will go into them for the benefit of the sick." The French relief group Médecins Sans Frontières (Doctors Without Borders) go to most dangerous places to render medical help. In Germany, Nazi doctors carried out Hitler's wish to get rid of the undesirables, the insane, the terminally ill, the handicapped, the elderly, the deformed children, and other "useless mouths." In the camps where I was incarcerated, there were infirmaries to which we all feared to be admitted. Germans patrolled through the infirmaries to pick up emaciated patients to be exterminated. They did not keep the oath never to be "unviolated." They had no conscience!

> *An unconscientious society will endow the human race with the ability to destroy itself. Without a moral foundation, all the energies, talents, and ideas might do more harm than good. It is the conscience that separates civilization from madness, the ability to think about right and wrong. Wiesenschaft, "Science without a conscience is the ruin of the soul."*
> (Rabelais, French humanist 1490-1553)

Q: *You saw so many people dying. Were you afraid of dying?*

DEATH

During the war, especially in camps, I had seen thousands of people dying, mainly from starvation. I often had to inhale the unmistakable smell of death, indescribably malodorous! I watched inmates wither, eyes shutting and the mouths contorting. I saw inmates moaning in pain, in loneliness, in the final stages of their expiration, breathing out the last prayers. Death was a frequent visitor in my life. I was constantly haunted by the shadow of death. My fear of death had been overcome, but my fear of dying remained.

Death is indeed a part of life. I have been close to death many times, but apparently, destiny snatched me from burning fires throughout the Holocaust.

I like to quote Winston Churchill, **"I am ready to meet my Maker. Whether my Maker is prepared for the ordeal of meeting me is another matter."**

Q: *You keep emphasizing the importance of education. There are many people in the U.S. who do very well without much of an education. You, too, Mr. Wiener, have somehow managed without a formal education. Many scientists, among them Jewish people like Einstein excelled even though they could not always be admitted to prestigious universities.*

EDUCATION

When you say, "do well," you are probably referring to doing well financially. This is possible in a free market economy. Also, somebody may be an heir to a fortune or be a winner in a lottery drawing. I am not referring to material needs; I am referring to the importance of acquiring knowledge to enhance a meaningful life. I shall repeat my conviction that, "Ignorance is indeed the enemy of mankind."

Because I had to stop going to school at the age of thirteen, I have always felt inferior educationally. When I come to share my story with high school students, I feel like joining them, even if they would make fun out of me.

Irrational conflicts of ideologies can only germinate in a landscape of ignorance. The emphasis should not be placed on indoctrination but on education. Education towards tolerance will bridge the widest chasms. To learn about somebody else's culture or religion is a source of enrichment that expands us rather than threatens.

In Poland, Jews strove to excel educationally hoping to have a better chance to be accepted by the gentile community. Some Jews understood that education would be a passport to freedom from social and religious codes that they had found to be too rigid and isolating. As a minority, Jews were restricted to engage in many areas of economic activities. Very few Jews could enroll in universities. Therefore, Jews had to dig inside themselves for energy, intelligence, creativity, and entrepreneurship. Not all knowledge is derived from books.

Eclectic education can transform anybody from an unhappy and destructive person into a happy and productive one because man is intrinsically malleable and flexible. A person is a piece of clay in the potter's hand to be molded as he pleases. Education is the most important component in that mold.

As a result of today's information revolution, education requirements are constantly increasing and changing. We have to be ready and able to upgrade and adapt to those new requirements. It is troubling to read that U.S. children average 900 hours a year in class and 1,023 hours in front of a television

We are challenged by a mounting deficit in Federal budgets, deficit in energy, foreign trade, health care, and social security, etc. In my observation, the biggest deficit is looming in education. I am quite often stunned by students' lack of knowledge of history.

Education is the information that can generate prevention. Creativity is the ultimate affirmation of life. Each individual should be given the freedom to pursue his intellectual aspirations and inherent talent.

Q: *I know that there were no videos when you were a kid. Where did you get entertainment?*

ENTERTAINMENT

In my hometown, there were no theaters for the performing arts, no museums for the visual arts, and only one movie house. I do not recall any theatrical troupes visiting our little town. I do recall once seeing a circus and clowns.

An ebullient cultural life prevailed in the many houses of worship, which served and nurtured the spiritual needs of the community. Faith and family were the epitome of the community. The majority were economically poor, but intellectually rich.

Q: *I have read that euthanasia was widely practiced in Germany. So, how do you feel about the vigils in the Schiavo case?*

EUTHANASIA

Terri Schiavo had been in a persistent vegetative state for fifteen years. Her family wished to prolong her life. Terri's husband, Michael Schiavo, who was the legal guardian, wanted his wife's life to be terminated and therefore, he had asked to have her feeding tubes withdrawn. It was euthanasia by omission, a heart wrenching case. Most Americans supported the court's decision to remove the feeding tube out of concern for Teri's quality of life. Those who were motivated by religious dogma or moral instinct would rather have her feeding tube reinserted. The outcome was up to the courts. Following that case in March 2005, I was witnessing a broad concern for the sanctity of life. The life of one individual was at stake and people cared.

If people all over the world would have shown as much concern for saving the life of millions during the Holocaust in 1939-45, or for the life of 800,000 Tutsis, and sympathetic Hutus, massacred in Rwanda in 1994, or recent massacres of 300,000 in the Sudan, millions of lives could have been saved. The Nazis cut off the flow of oxygen to a million-and-a-half Jewish children during the Holocaust. There were no vigils then.

Tubes that convey blood to the brain are the same in all human beings.

Q: *Did you keep faith and hope in the camps?*

FAITH AND HOPE

Yes indeed. Saying good-bye to our father before fleeing Chrzanów, I recall him saying, "God, as long as I have to be separated from my precious family, it is not going to defeat me, because I know that you are on my side."

When the Nazis shot my father and let him bleed to death, a Pole passing by at the scene, who knew my father from business, offered water to my father who graciously declined it while uttering a sigh of his last words, "God gave my soul and God takes my soul."

He simply placed his fate in God's hands. His belief was tested, confirmed, and not changed. If my father had not been such an ardent faithful man, the agony would have been immeasurably harder to bear.

The Pole told my stepmother about that incident one year after the murder of my father.

In times of despair, genuine believers had hoped that God would ultimately come to their rescue. God is omniscient and omnipotent. That pious environment which permeated my parents' home left a profound imprint on me.

I had six million reasons not to have hope. Hope can be defined as expectations, self-delusion, optimism, and obviously faith. Despite all of the adversities in my path, I believed that God did not want me to live in perpetual pain. I hoped that God would compensate my bitter adolescent years with sweet ones in my adulthood.

I considered myself to be innocent and questioned, like the biblical Job, why God let me be inflicted with so much misery and pain. Moses debated God, so did I. Pope Benedict XVI on his visit to Auschwitz (5/29/2006) questioned God in his prayer, "Why, Lord, did you remain silent?" Moses asked God why he was chosen to lead; I asked God why he had chosen me to suffer. However, I always recalled the reference in Psalms (34:20) that God will eventually deliver the righteous of all inflictions. I had hope that the future would be better than the present.

One of my room inmates, who had been raised in a very pious family, after being mercilessly beaten by a guard, told me," Today is the end of my faith. What is happening here refutes the belief that God is a merciful God. How can God see me suffering and not stop the cruelty of that guard beating me so wickedly? I feel abandoned by God and by mankind."

I asked the man, "If there was no God, why have the Jewish people struggled for so many centuries to keep their faith? Isn't that faith what buoyed the spirit of the Jewish people in times of oppression? I just did not see the point of losing faith at that point!"

He kept silent. I was much younger than that man was and knew very little about anything. I just remember asking him, "Are you sure that you have reached the final conclusion? Do you have an ultimate and philosophical explanation? Just because God didn't answer your prayers this time, is this an absolute proof that God does not exist? If you are not able to discern God's existence, how sure can you be that there is no God?"

Today, I see that there are many levels of understanding any phenomenon in life. Theology, philosophy, chemistry, physics, and biochemistry, etc. try to explain life from their own perspective. In reality, none has the ultimate answer and apparently never will. Despite all the benefits and conveniences that the modern and secular world provides, it does not have all the answers. Our faith does not require us to close our minds; you may still ponder about life's complexity. As long as there is no absolute compelling evidence to the veracity of any of the contemporary theories, I have to adhere to my faith in the Providence. Divine grace was probably capable of awarding man a soul at some stage of his physical development.

Fear of beatings by the Nazi guards seemed to be greater than fear of heaven. Still, I have never renounced my faith in God. I have protested his silence, but my anger rose up in faith and not outside of it. Sometimes I wonder why! However, it has always been my perception that living organisms are so inexplicably complex that there must have been a higher authority in control and design. Jeremiah compares an atheist to a tree planted in the desert.

I had a friend who had stopped observing the Jewish tradition and rituals for several years and then returned to the folds of his religion. To my asking for an explanation he replied, "I had a lot of fun with my lover and then my crop failed. I decided to go back to my wife. Her embrace makes me feel more secure; she makes my life more meaningful."

I wondered why God did not send upon Hitler of Germany a variety of plagues as he had sent on Pharaoh of Egypt. After God's punishment, the Hebrew slaves were released, and could return to the Promised Land. I was thirsty to experience the mercy of God, but God kept testing me in my traumatic trials.

Throughout history, Jews could avoid persecution by converting to Christianity, or in the Middle-Ages to Islam. During the Holocaust, there was no such escape available. Jews who intermarried, Jews who have not practiced Judaism, and converted Jews; all faced the ultimate fate of annihilation.

In psychiatry, there is a certain condition known as "delusion of reprieve." The condemned man immediately before execution gets the illusion that he might be reprieved at the very last minute. In forced labor camps, the secularists clung to shreds of hope that the free world would free them from slavery. The religious Jews believed to the last minute that God would come to their rescue. They were armed with a conviction of the existence of an omnipotent and benevolent God. I remembered Isaiah (41.10), "Fear thou not; for I am with thee. Be not dismayed, for I am thy God. I will strengthen thee. Yea, I will help thee."

I kept the faith and the faith kept me.

Rabbi Harold Kushner was motivated to write his best-selling book, *When Bad Things Happen to Good People* after his fourteen-year-old son had died of a rare disease.

In the wake of the terrible events of September 11, 2001, people in the street and television interviewers asked him, "Where was God? How could God let this happen?" Rabbi Kushner's response was, as cited in his recent book, "The Lord is my Shepherd. God's promise was never that life would be fair. God's promise was that, when we had to confront the unfairness of life, we would not have to do it alone because He would be with us. His presence lessens our anxiety."

So do I question why was I orphaned at the age of thirteen, subjugated at the age of fifteen to malice treatment, and losing hundreds of relatives in the Holocaust? I needed an explanation! Why were the German murderers not stopped or punished for brutally violating the sixth commandment, "You shall not murder?"

I am angry with God! However, to be angry with God means to be in a relationship with God. I feel God in my fury, and love God in my bewilderment.

God set the rainbow in the heavens as a reminder of His promise that no matter how hard it rained, sooner or later the rain would stop and the sun would come out again. When I was tormented, alienated, and bloodied, I felt not alone when I recalled the twenty-third Psalm, "I will fear no evil for Thou art with me." My belief in God and that he was with me in my torment alleviated my pain, and my suffering. "Faith is the substance of things hoped for, the evidence of things not seen." (Hebrews II:I.) Faith provides hope to people who endure hardship in their daily life, people who might otherwise be tempted to despair.

I have reconciled with the fact that I shall never understand God. I do not claim to know the ways of Providence. Certainly, God works in mysterious ways, but I also believe that God has a reason for the way He acts. Albert Einstein, a great scientist in the history of our species was a religious person. He did not observe every tenet of Judaism but believed in God. He realized that his Theory of Relativity had the limit of his mind's capacity and there must be a divine infinite power, a deity that sets rules for everything in the universe. Einstein's scientific brilliance didn't promote godless materialism. I am not qualified to question Einstein's theory, and I am not in a position to nullify the validity of millenniums of believers in God's supremacy.

The Torah embodies beautiful precepts and so are the Bible and the Koran. It is the interpreters of God's word, by the faithful and heretics alike that are causing so much friction and hatred among people.

God is a spirit. He is infinite, eternal, and unchangeable in His wisdom, power, holiness, justice, goodness, and truth. God had been testing me but I can't test God. I am unable to understand the workings of God, the mind of God, or to explain fully life's complexities.

Q: *Are you willing to forgive the Germans?*

FORGIVENESS

I am ready to forgive the German who knocked out my teeth if he would acknowledge and show remorse for his brutal action. However, I am not able to forgive the Germans for the suffering and death they inflicted on my family, relatives, and all the other victims who are no longer here to talk for themselves. I feel that I am not at liberty to redeem the sin of genocide. I think that the Germans must continue to reflect deeply with humility upon the suffering they and their forbearers brought upon millions of innocent people. Germany's World War II record of atrocities should never be downplayed. It is a festering wound in Nazi Germany's records.

I am eagerly willing to reconcile with contemporary Germans because the majority of Germans living today were not alive during the Holocaust. Thus, they could not have hurt me, and there is nothing for me to forgive them.

An Israeli Jew, with many relatives who had perished in the Holocaust, several years ago married Kathrine Himmler, a niece of Heinrich Himmler, who was responsible for the death of millions. Kathrine was accepted and embraced by her husband's family, as reflected in her book, *The Himmler Brothers*. Collective guilt is always unjustifiable.

Reconciliation between the Jewish people and the Germans is desirable and practical. The post-Holocaust German governments had confronted and objectively judged Germany's wartime conduct. Konrad Adenauer, West German chancellor, accepted responsibility for the crimes committed by Nazi Germany and agreed to pay a symbolic compensation to the Nazis' victims. Reconciliation does not necessitate forgiveness, although it is difficult. Reconciliation works to conquer hatred. Nevertheless, it would be unacceptable that anyone should escape accountability for an act of wanton cruelty. The murderers of the Holocaust must face a moment of truth. Nobody should shield murderers from justice.

I am seeking justice not vengeance, although my pain and grief has been unending. There is an aphorism, "Justice may involve hurting someone because the person deserves to be hurt, but revenge involves hurting someone because it makes you feel better to hurt him or her." Revenge is subjective; justice is objective. Revenge is personal. Justice is procedural.

Q: *We are always told that Americans are sent overseas to fight for our freedom. What does freedom mean to you?*

FREEDOM

Sometime ago, I spoke to a group of American World War II veterans and this is what I said, "You are awarding me with a unique opportunity to thank you, in person, for liberating me in 1945. You were fighting for freedom, a commodity that could not be attained or protected without sacrifice. You ennobled humanity with your valor. I will never be able to repay my debt to you. Even though I, personally, was liberated by the Russians, you were fighting the same enemy, the Nazis. I shall forever be grateful to the U.S. for enabling me to live in this land of freedom and opportunity. The U.S. is still the beacon of pluralism and tolerance. I celebrate the Fourth of July, Independence Day, every day. During the Holocaust, **I had the freedom to die but not to live!** The liberty granted to me in this country is the antidote of everything I was deprived of in my teens. At the age of thirteen, I was robbed of my freedom to live in peace when the German armies invaded and occupied Poland. The Nazis took away my freedom to worship, to go to school and study, to move freely, to associate freely, and to work freely. They violated my basic human rights and needs. At the age of fifteen, I was deported to slave labor camps in desolate places where smiling children, gracious women, meadows or flowers were not a part of the landscape. I did not have a book to read, nor a pencil to write; nothing of the kind that might have enhanced my mind. Hard labor, starvation, torrential brutality, torture, and the threat of annihilation was the daily menu during three years of my incarceration.

I did not fight on the battlefronts as many of you did. The Nazis subjugated me. For over five years, I was targeted daily with atrocities, not for my transgressions but for whom I was, a Jew conceived by the Nazis as pernicious to the social order and purity of the Arian race. The Nazis considered themselves superior and Jews, gypsies, Slavs, Blacks and many others were noxious and Untermentchen, subhuman and not worthy of freedom. The goose-stepping German soldiers' song echoed their beliefs Heute Deutschland, morgen die ganze Welt, Today Germany, tomorrow the entire world or Deutschland, Deutschland ueber alles, Germany, Germany is above everything. All decent people are worthy to live in freedom.

Let the Bells of Freedom Ring!

Q: *You probably appreciate the abundance of food in this country. Do you say grace before and after each meal? I do!*

GRACE—FOOD TO BE BLESSED UPON

I commend you for that. As a young child, as soon as I knew how to utter a few words, I was taught to say grace before a meal and different blessings before the intake of any food, or beverages between meals. Eating the food of a new season required the citation of the Shechianu, "Blessed are you, O Lord, King of the Universe, Who have kept us alive, and have preserved us, to reach this period." Eating without reciting grace was considered a sin, which might be deemed as too rigid. However, retrospectively, it seems to me a method of sowing the seeds of appreciation for food for which the farmer toiled the soil, and God provided light, heat, and water, etc.

A festive meal was an integral part of every Sabbath and holidays. It always started with a blessing while rising with a small cup of wine in hand. During the meal, between the courses, we sung in unison songs of thanksgiving for the food, for the Sabbath, for the holidays, and for sustenance that God granted us. The meal at the table was always concluded with "Birchat Hamazon," Grace for the consumed food. I do not recall ever seeing somebody eating in the street. It is written in the Talmud that a person who eats in the street resembles a dog.

My stepmother Rachel was a wonderful cook; every meal was a feast, especially on holidays. My father never failed to thank his wife for having prepared a delicious meal. For us, the children, it was not just a matter of manners to thank mom, but we were religiously obligated to do so.

Q: *Mr. Wiener, you are a man who went through so much in his life. Still you seem to be in good health. Am I right? If I am right, is it your lifestyle? Is it your philosophy, your genes, or your faith? There must be a sensible reason for your longevity. I also read that many survivors died soon after the liberation.*

HEALTH DURING THE GERMAN OCCUPATION, INCARCERATION AND ITS AFTERMATH

Frankly, I have never expected to reach the age of eighty, as I am now. During the Holocaust, everybody's health was adversely affected due to food scarcity, lack of proper medical care, and frequent physical abuse inflicted by the Nazis. Food was rationed to the general population while goods and local produce were diverted to Nazi warehouses. Basic staples such as eggs or sugar were obtainable on the black market at inflated prices that very few could afford, and if caught by the police, the buyer and seller faced severe punishment.

I remember having an infectious disease at the age of fourteen. My immune system weakened due to lack of vitamins and minerals. If you cheat the body of vitamin rich food, then you are on a disease-producing diet!

Later on, when I was put behind barbed wire in forced labor and concentration camps, I was beaten, wounded, and starved which left many physical and mental scars. Skin peeling and skin rashes or pus accumulation as a result of silicon deficiencies, were very painful. My legs were so atrophied that the fingers of one of my hands could reach around one of my legs. I never received any medical treatment. The German doctors, instead of treating the ill, they ill-treated them. Some scars and scabs will stay for the rest of my life. When I was hospitalized in June 1945, Russian military doctors gave me a thorough examination and told me, "Sorry, young man, your life span will last no longer than two years." I was then an eighteen-year-old adolescent, and I am now an eighty-year-old man. Apparently, those medical doctors erred, and probably are dead by now, but I am still here. I wonder sometimes, ironically, if suffering had promoted my longevity.

For many years after the war, I was a very sickly young man. The residues of the war hindered my recovery. The most troubling ailment had been for many years my inability to digest common staples of food such as meat, and dairy products, etc. My stomach rejected and ejected the meals that I prepared, or was served. Many Holocaust survivors died soon after the war when it became too difficult for their digestive system to assimilate the rich food their bodies were weaned off of during the war. The metabolism, attuned to 500 calories a day, could not handle a "normal" intake of food. In the Bergen-Belsen concentration camp alone, fourteen thousand inmates died shortly after being liberated by the British army. For many years, I had been seeking and getting medical treatment; different diagnoses and a variety of medications were prescribed which did not provide much relief.

In 1953, Jacob Grabois, a co-worker, in Israel, once said to me, "It pains me to see a young man to be absent from work so often due to illness. Perhaps if you adopt my lifestyle it might help you, as it has helped me." Grabois invited me to visit with him. He and his wife (they had no children) lived in a little house, that was modestly furnished, with an adjacent large garden. That garden yielded a crop of almost all the basic foods that the Grabois family consumed. No fertilizers were used—just a large compost dumpster, at one corner of the garden, contributed to the fertile soil. While savoring a delicious vegetarian dinner, Jacob Grabois told us his life story and what motivated him to become a vegan.

As a young student in France, he became very concerned about his health, and his life expectancy. Since his father and his siblings died of cancer, he feared that the same fate awaited him. He studied the causes of diseases and eventually adopted a new lifestyle and a vegan diet. In 1958, Jacob Grabois was diagnosed with colon cancer. He did not seek conventional medical help but chose to fast for forty days (he abstained from solid food for forty days but did drink water and juices from the fifth day of fasting) He lived another forty-two years after being diagnosed with cancer. He died at the age of ninety-two.

I adopted, to a degree, his lifestyle and it seems to have worked for me, too. As soon as I avoided meat, fish, and most dairy products, my health improved. Some friends ridiculed my weird behavior. Once I was invited for dinner. The hostess, Mrs.Schnitzer, left. I asked her, "Where are you going to?" She replied, "To my yard to bring some grass for you."

I became a strict vegetarian and a teetotaler in 1969. I eat some dairy products but mainly fruits. I had been in relatively good health until the year 2005 when I had a colon surgery resection (due to cancer). Otherwise, I have been content with all parts of my body and so are my female friends.

I fast sometimes just to let my digestive system rest for a day. I feel that putting away the knife and fork for a day or two, I am postponing the digging of my grave.

I have also learned from the following renowned people.

Albert Einstein said, "It is my view that the vegetarian manner of living, by its purely physical effect on the human temperament would most beneficially influence the lot of mankind."

Benjamin Franklin said, "Flesh eating is unprovoked murder."

Pythagorus, "As long as we continue to be ruthless destroyers of lower living beings, we will never know health or peace. For as long as we massacre animals, we will kill each other. Indeed, those who sow the seed of murder and pain cannot reap and love."

Roseau, "Meat-eating animals are generally more cruel and violent than herbivores; therefore a vegetarian diet would produce a more compassionate person."

George Bernard Shaw said, "We are sick of war! We don't want to fight and yet we gorge ourselves on the dead. I look my age. It is the other people who look older. That's what happens when people eat corpses." Shaw lived until the age of ninety-four. A young reporter who interviewed George Bernard Shaw on his ninetieth birthday party said, "Mr. Shaw, I hope to interview you again ten years from now." Mr. Shaw's reply to the reporter was, "I don't see why not; you, young man, look pretty healthy to me."

Henry Thoreau wrote, "I have no doubt that it is a part of destiny of the human race, in its gradual improvement, to leave off eating animals."

If everybody would become a vegan or a vegetarian, there could be an abundance of food for every living soul on this planet, because cattle need arable land and water ten times as much as humans do.

Q: *Why was Hitler such a vile anti-Semite? I know that he hated many other groups, but he considered the Jews to be his sworn enemy. Did Anti-Semitism start in Germany?*

HITLER'S ANTI-SEMITISM

The term Anti-Semitism was coined in Germany in 1879 by Wilhelm Marr. Jews were hated because they were considered capitalist but also because they were communists; they were too religious but also because they were too secular. Jews refused to assimilate, but also Jews were too eager to assimilate. Jews were stingy but they were also ostentatious spenders, and so on. Anti-Semitism has always been a mental disease but contagious and became endemic at certain times in history. For two millenniums, Jews were blamed for the killing of Jesus. The 1965 Second Vatican Council document, *Nostra Aetate*, rejected collective Jewish responsibility for Jesus' death. So should all the above unreasonable accusations be rejected!

Hitler's damaged mind was impervious to reason and lucidity. He was not amenable to a change of heart. To fight the Jews became a duty, rather than a choice. Hitler harbored an incurable disease. He professed a grudging admiration for Jewish clannishness, which he believed had given Jews superior intelligence. He was envious of the Jewish intellectual and cultural success. He resented the fact that so many nations collapsed and disappeared from the world scene, but the Jew who had no state of its own (remember this was prior to the re-establishment of the State of Israel, 1948) survived. He fraudulently portrayed the Jew as an enemy of the German culture. The tenacity and resourcefulness of the Jewish people frustrated Hitler and he decided to abort the pregnancy of a community's potential.

On January 30, 1939, Hitler said, "Today I wish to be a prophet once more. Should international Jewry, inside and outside Europe, succeed once more in plunging the nations into war, the result will not be the Bolshevization of the earth and through it the victory of Jewry, but the annihilation of the Jewish race in Europe."

Anti-Semitic violence began with Jews as targets, but like untreated cancer, metastasized and infected many other groups under the Nazi occupation. Hermann Göring (Hitler's *Reichsmarshall*, Reich Marshal) had become alarmed when the vandalism and looting against Jewish targets spread to non-Jewish targets. The brown-shirted violent youth became a symbol of rudeness feared by ordinary Germans. It seemed, at times, that the Nazi government was losing control on its fanatic elements.

Hitler believed that the purity of the Germanic-Aryan race had been compromised through a "blending process" such as inter-marriage with Jews. Hitler's logic of pseudoscientific eugenics is just twisted and baseless. He advocated preserving uncontaminated stocks of Aryan blood. Hitler adopted de Gobineau's thesis that "contamination" resulted from inter-breeding between the white, namely the Nordic race and other races.

Paradoxically, Count Joseph Arthur de Gobineau wrote (Essay on the inequality of Human Races) about the Jews, "A people that succeeded in everything it undertook, a free, strong, and intelligent people... Had given many learned men to the world." The same people were thrown into darkness by the Nazis. Hitler portrayed the Jews in negative light, according to his own vision, and he would not budge from that image he had created. His prejudice portrayed the war as an apocalyptic battle between Aryans and Jews.

In the Diaspora, the dispersion of Jews constituted a tiny minority everywhere. When Hitler came to power in 1933, there were only 500,000 Jews living in Germany within a population of sixty-five million; less than 1 percent of the population. The percentage of the Jewish eminence in professions, Jewish professors who enjoyed great prestige in arts and science was about 20 percent. In World War I,

92,000 Jews had served in the German army of whom 35,000 were decorated for heroism and 12,000 had been killed in action. All these contributions to Germany's prominence didn't matter in Hitler's eyes of hatred and fascism. He initiated the abuse of the German Jewish citizens as soon as he reached power and later on he pursued racial exclusion and eventually mass murder.

In April 1933, any governmental employee had to sign the following statement: "I declare officially herewith: I do not know of any circumstance—despite careful scrutiny—that may justify the presumption that I am not of Aryan descent; in particular, none of my paternal or maternal parents, or grandparents, was at any time of the Jewish faith. I am fully aware of the fact that I expose myself to prosecution and dismissal if this declaration proves untrue."

Mixed couples were humiliated by being forced to wear a sign saying, *Ich bin ein Rasseschänder*—"I am a race defiler."

Karl Marx (1818-1883) although a Jew by birth, was baptized. Marx, who wrote the Communist Manifesto in 1848 *Das Kapital*, was considered to be the founder of the modern left; socialism and communism. This gave Hitler a reason to hate ALL Jews because he opposed Marxism. This made as much sense as Charles E. Coughlin, the Detroit anti-Semitic priest who asserted that the Germans' violence was a defense mechanism against Jewish sponsored communism. In both cases, it was just breathtaking insanity!

Mayer A. Rothschild (1743-1812), a Frenchman and a Jew by birth, who was a prominent and a successful banker in Europe, gave a pretext to Hitler to aver that ALL Jews were capitalists; that they pulled the strings of the world's financial markets. The Jewish people might have been rich in culture and rich in history, but most Jews, especially in East Europe, were not wealthy. Many lived below the poverty level. Hitler deemed the Jewish-capitalists a menace to Germany's survival. The Rothschild family and other well-to-do Jews had been known as philanthropists, still Jews were often stereotyped as parsimonious.

As a boy, Albert Einstein's teacher at the Luitpold Gymnasium in Munich, encouraged him to leave the school because his indolence affected the diligence of his classmates, and that he would never make a success of anything. Given a chance that his genius was overpowering, Einstein was recognized by the scientific world as a symbol of genius.

Nuclear power, television, telecommunication, computers, and satellites all owe their invention to Einstein's theory of General Relativity. Had Einstein missed the opportunity to escape Germany, he probably would have perished in the Holocaust! The Nazis classified Albert Einstein as a subhuman like all other Jews. Isn't it ridiculous?

Jews were also a biological challenge to blood purity of the German race, polluting its biological heritage. Were these logical reasons for hatred and eventual genocide of European Jewry? Was there any basis for the characterization of the Jews as the "cosmopolitan enemy who would stab Germany in the back?" Sweeping guilt by association is essentially abhorrent. It mounts on an empire of lies.

Germans who have never dealt with or even met a Jewish person accepted Hitler's version as a fact. The German civilized society slid into uncivilized behavior. It became a popularized myth—a legend. The German youth indoctrinated by Nazism from an early age joined the lynching mobs. They had no access to books or objective information, other than those that had been approved by their government. Their minds had been poisoned by hate. I believe that many decent Germans were just caught up in the current of propagandized hatred for non-Aryans.

Anti-Semitism is also implicit racism as manifested by Hitler in the 1936 Olympic Games. When Jesse Owens won four gold medals, Hitler said to Babldur von Schirach, the Nazi Youth Leader, "The Americans should be ashamed of themselves to have Negroes win their medals for them. I won't shake hands with this Negro."

Hitler, unable to face his own inadequacies, looked for scapegoats and targets to attack and blame. An oppressive government such as Nazi Germany must have an enemy to unify the populace.

Anti-Semitism fails the enlightenment and modernity of cotemporary societies in a free world. It contaminates every crevice of human dignity.

Q: *Watching documentaries, Hitler in his appearances and in his speeches seemed to be a little bit emotionally unstable, perhaps insane. What do you think?*

HITLER'S INSANITY

Yes, indeed. In the year 2000, the FBI declassified documents pertaining to Hitler. In one of the documents, Dr. Ferdinand Sauerbach, Hitler's personal physician in 1937, stated that the German dictator was showing signs of growing megalomania. Hitler was mentally unbalanced in any clinical sense. He may have been a genius, but insane at the same time.

Dr. Theodore Morell, one of Hitler's physicians, prescribed for Hitler an array of seventy-three medications. It included tonics, vitamins, sedatives, stimulants, hypnotics, hormones, a variety of opium, steroids such as cortisone, cocaine, methamphetamine, etc. All those had a deleterious effect on his ability to judge and to reason. Hitler's irritability and restlessness were reflected in his appearances when his cheeks flushed with rage, when his body trembled, and when his eyes popped out.

When the German defeat became inevitable, Hitler instructed the German military to destroy the bridges, the railroads, the factories, and the lines of food production in Germany. He insisted that anything short of absolute victory would put Germany in mortal danger. Hitler said, "The German people do not deserve to live if Germany was defeated." Luckily enough most generals, at that point, no longer carried out the *Führer's* orders and thus prevented Germany from complete devastation. This fanaticism unmasks Hitler's true character. He was an opportunist rather than a nationalist.

Self-conscious geniuses, such as Hitler, want all their ideas to be carried out, and they regard anybody else's ideas as unacceptable. Rivals must be eliminated. In 1944, Ernst Röhm, the head of the SA *Sturmabteilungen*, (Storm Detachments) was killed by Hitler's order. Hitler's "superior" ideas had to be adopted in every case. As the *Führer* of Germany, he was just omnipotent.

Hitler was not capable of having a friendly conversation with anybody. On the other hand, his oratorical ability anesthetized the German public despite his ruthlessness. Hitler had a super inferiority complex. In November 1937, Hitler said at a party rally, "This is the miracle of our times that you have found me among the millions.... That is Germany's fortune." (E.H.Schwaab, *Hitler's' Mind: A Plunge into Madness,* p.29). Like in a classic Greek tragedy, the hero rises to great heights, only to fall by his own hubris.

People cannot choose the time or place of their birth and can never control the timing of their last breath (excluding suicide). Hitler felt that his birth was a miracle and he was empowered to be in control of the world. The hunger for recognition motivated Hitler to seek glory aggressively and kill those who disrespected his ambitions.

Q: *You said that Hitler believed the Germans to be a Master Race. Was it a theory? Was it scientifically proven? I would appreciate if you could elaborate. I am very interested.*

HITLER'S MASTER RACE

The Nazis attempted to create a master race by wiping out all of these so-called "defective traits." In his speeches, Hitler emphasized the strength of the German people and reviled the weaknesses of other nationalities. "Look at our splendid youth; I do not want anything weak in them. One must defend the strong that are menaced by their inferiors. A state which, in a period of race pollution, devotes itself to caring for its best racial elements must someday become the lord of the earth." The populace will not be multicolored, not multiethnic—just monochromatic with blue eyes and blond hair. There was a conspicuous condescension toward any non-German and in some cases hatred with genocidal aims.

On August 22, 1939, just several days prior to the German invasion of Poland, Hitler gave orders to his military commanders at Obersaltzberg, "Send to death mercilessly and without compassion, men, women and children of Polish derivation and language. Only thus shall we gain Lebensraum, (living space) which we need."

Mein Kampf, Hitler's mendacious biography is mostly plagiarized. He was neither a scholar nor an autodidact. The quality of thought and writing does not rise to the level of a literary novice. He read a lot but misinterpreted what he had read. Hitler was narrow-minded and irrational. He wrote vapid abstractions. His heartless and muddy ideas were written with bloody hands. Reading *Mein Kampf,* (My fight), would not shed much light on Hitler's understanding of the world he lived in. Hitler's broad-based intolerance asserted that racial struggle transcends class, religions, cultural, and economical differences. It is tragic that so many Germans were amenable to Hitler's ideology.

Hitler believed that the main function of a state was to place the capable personalities to high positions of authority. The majority should not decide who should rule (a democratic theory), but the superior minds should decide. Hitler saw himself as an exceptional figure, a genius, which definitely he was not. He was a bully, and bullies are sometimes cowards rather than courageous. Hitler presented himself as a gifted personality when he was confirmed by the party (in 1926) as *Führer* (leader). A cult honoring this theoretical gift prevailed during the Third Reich.

Young impressionable Germans were indoctrinated into thinking that they were born with innate superiority and could be a source of pride for their nation by joining the Hitler *Jugend* (Hitler's Youth), a regiment imbued with patriotism and antagonism towards non-Aryan. Textbooks were brainwashing German students against foreigners while whitewashing German's historical failures. The Nazi government had a big role in approving those textbooks.

Teaching hatred to young people becomes an ineradicable cancer. When beliefs and images are uncontested or even dominant within a given society, individuals typically come to accept them as self-evident truths. Phrases such as "Master Race" or "defective traits" become part of the apparatus of the mind and generate expectations and behavior accordingly. It becomes incumbent upon the "Master Race" to inexorably kill the "Defective Races."

Non-Aryan Catholics were shunned by their Aryan co-religionist attending the sanctuary of the same church. "All who are not of good race in this world are chaff," Hitler wrote in *Mein Kampf* (p.269).

Of the estimated five-and-a-half-million Russian soldiers who reached German prisoner-of-war camps, just over a million survived the war. The struggle with Germany cost the Soviet Union more than twenty-seven million of its people. These killing were carried out for pragmatic and political motives to be rid of the burden of prisoners, to destroy future generations of enemies, and to increase German living space. In the Nazis' eyes, these were indubitably inferior peoples.

In February 2005, the UN and many other countries commemorated the sixtieth anniversary of the Liberation of Auschwitz by the Russian troops. Ceremonies took place in Auschwitz and tributes were paid to the victims of the Holocaust in many parliaments over the globe. I was palpably disgusted reading that in Germany, the National Democrats (neo-Nazis) walked out of the parliamentary chamber during a ceremony to honor the victims of Auschwitz, saying that they would honor only German victims of World War II. What a revulsion to the memory of Nazis' victims.

In 1920, Karl Binding and psychiatrist Alfred Hoche coined the phrase "*lebensunwertes Leben*" in their book, *Die Freigabe der Vernichtung lebensunwerten lebens* (Lifting control on the destruction of life unworthy of life). They advocated that society should terminate a life when it becomes a burden to society; a theory that became the Nazi regime's rational for euthanasia.

Gnadentod (mercy killing) took place in local hospitals and in nursing homes of the mentally ill, in Poznań. Constant executions, on behalf of eugenics and euthanasia took place not just in the occupied land of Europe but also in Germany proper.

German researchers found new evidence that at least 200,000 disabled, mentally ill, and other institutional patients who were deemed to be inferior were killed by the Germans. They executed Hitler's program to purify, as he saw it, the German race. Medical staff in hospitals, located in Germany, Austria, Poland and the Czech Republic, used gas, drugs or starvation to murder those "worthless lives." In September 2003, German Culture Minister, Christina Weiss, said at a news conference, "We know that these crimes were meant to be kept secret. The relatives of the victims received fake letters of condolence. The doctors-in-charge worked under false names. All those delegated to give loving care caused death by manslaughter, fraud, and assault."

We know that Hitler was bent on creating the empire of the master race and perceived himself as Germany's messiah. Hitler lived with a vision, a goal to conquer the world, and to impose its pernicious system. His bellicosity was a by-product of a fanatical ideology. Hitler's path ran through Europe but it would not have stopped there if the Allies had not won the war.

The Nazis adopted Charles Darwin's theory that all creatures, including humans, evolved by selection. In *On the Origin of Species* published in 1859, Darwin argues that the diverse organisms descended from a common ancestor. The weak and imperfect have to be eliminated, and only the most superior should reproduce. He envisioned a world occupied by perfect homo sapiens. Religion was nonsense, and the idea that all men were created equal contradicted the nature of nature, because God was nature and nature abhorred imperfection. It was difficult to argue with the brainwashed Germans.

To propagate Aryan traits of the Master Race, the SS devised the *Lebensborn* (spring of life) clinics throughout Germany, where women, mostly single, gave birth in secret to children fathered by senior SS officers. To be accepted into the *Lebensborn*, pregnant women had to have blonde hair, blue eyes, and no genetic disorders. The women had to swear loyalty to Nazism, indoctrinated with Hitler's ideology. Many of those children, when they grew up, did not prove to be specially talented or immune from disabilities or illnesses.

Heinrich Himmler, a leader of the SS *Schutzstaffel* (Protection Squad) was instrumental in establishing *Dachau* in March 1933, the first concentration camp in Germany. German communists were the first to be incarcerated there. Himmler's instructions enabled the SS guards to terrorize their prisoners at will. They became soul-less killers. He regarded the camps as a necessary institution where German's enemies, undesirables, and disabled persons should be cut off from the rest of national society.

Arthur Comte de Gobineau, a Frenchman, in his 1855 "Essay on the Inequality of the Human Races," maintained that races are innately unequal, and that the white races, especially the Aryan ones, are at the pinnacle of a hierarchical racial pyramid.

The Nazis believed that exercising power entails contempt for those over whom power is being exercised. Intolerance and self-righteousness was the order of the day. The cruelty of Hitler and the Nazis had ineluctably changed the face of the German people.

There are two races of people in this world: the race of the decent person and the race of the indecent person. Both are found everywhere. They are present in all groups of society. If every person on this planet shares the same beating rhythm of the heart, the same red color of the blood streaming in the veins, then the commonality of the human race transcends all the differences among man and peoples. Anthropology has proven that peoples and races are fundamentally very much alike. We have to focus on the common denominator that characterizes all of us human rather than on our differences. Fascination with ourselves prevents us from seeing the beauty of others. Pluralism may be dealt with by valuing each other and discovering each other.

There is a certain genius in all of us. We are like diamonds. Every stone is different. The quality and flaws keep changing. The hardest stone becomes a shimmering diamond if cut and shaped correctly. If a person breaks out of all the barriers imposed upon him, he will thrive and carry others with him.

Bloodshed among nations, races, and ethnic groups, etc. will end only when everyone sees one another as equal humans. Each person has equal worth. Reconciliation rather than polarization among ethnic and sectarian groups is the solution. Whatever our religious and ethnic differences are, we are one human family with a common destiny. Every person in every community should have a real opportunity to utilize his or her ability.

The major cause for evil is the idea that humans are divided into races and some races, such as the German race, are naturally superior to others. The Nazis considered themselves to be the *crème de la crème* of the human race. This fallacy contradicts the scientific findings that racial differences are biologically minimal. The variation among individuals of the same race is far greater than the variations between the races. To murder others over different ethnicity or culture is tragic. In fact, there is hardly any person in Europe who does not have at least one hybrid among his or ancestors. The theory of a pure-breed race is questionable. Racism equals fanaticism and the existence of a master race is just a myth.

Q: *I have read somewhere that Hitler was gay. Was he really?*

HITLER'S SEXUALITY

In *The Hidden Hitler*, Lothar Machtan writes that Hitler ordered the killing of several high-ranking Nazis to protect his homosexuality. Ernst Rohm, the head of the *Sturmabteilungen*, (Strom Detachments-brown-shirts) was gay and tried to blackmail Hitler by threatening to reveal his homosexuality. Hitler supposedly ordered "The night of the long knives" in 1934, when 100 of his most embarrassing and threatening followers were purged. Even the Nazi persecution of gay men, many of whom were sent to concentration camps, was a function of Hitler's self-hatred and effort to disguise his own sexual preferences, Machtan argues.

Q: *You bemoaned the fact that your family members who perished in the Holocaust never had a funeral nor a grave. I could empathize with you, because my brother drowned and his body was never recovered. My mother has never stopped crying over it, and the fact that she cannot even visit his grave. Isn't it ironic that Hitler did not have a funeral either, and he has no grave?*

HITLER'S SUICIDE

Hitler committed suicide on April 30, 1945 (eight days prior to Germany's surrender) by shooting himself through the mouth. His body was dumped by the Russians in the backyard of the chancellery, and doused with petroleum and burned.

You are right! Hitler never had a funeral just as millions of his victims had none.

Q: *Mr. Wiener, you shared with us your personal experience during the Holocaust. Could you please give a more general background of the Holocaust? I read Night by Elie Wiesel. He is from Rumania, which was much later impacted than Poland where you come from.*

HOLOCAUST

This presentation has a time limit, but I shall try to be concise as much as possible.

Hitler initiated the persecution of unimaginable proportions against the German Jews. Later on, he decided that not only Germany should become completely "*judenrein*," cleansed of Jews, but the whole of Europe. Hitler and his cohorts introduced a vengeful and violent xenophobia against the Jewish people that eventually led to the Holocaust. The unchecked evil became a prelude to genocide.

There were no violent confrontations, no warfare, and no reason for retributions. The Jews in Germany and in the occupied lands by Germany were neither rebellious nor obstreperous. They were overwhelmingly passive and mostly resigned to the danger that encircled them.

On October 8, 1942, addressing the National Socialist party at the Munich *Löwenbräukeller*, Hitler said, "People have laughed at my prophecies. Countless numbers of those who laughed are no longer laughing today. And those who are still laughing may not be laughing for long." By the time of Hitler's boastful statement, the chimneys of the crematoriums were smoking, day and night. In February 1945, three months before German's capitulation, Hitler told Martin Bormann, a Nazi leader, "For us this has been an essential process of disinfection, which we have prosecuted to its ultimate limit."

Hitler initiated the Holocaust as "*die Endlösung der Judenfrage*" the Final Solution to the Jewish question, because he realized that the entire previous attempt to eradicate the Jewish people by conversion and assimilation had not materialized. The implementation of the "Final Solution" was discussed at the *Wannsee* (suburb outside Berlin) Conference on 1/20/42. That meeting was attended by five members of the *Gestapo*, including Adolf Eichman.

Addressing SS commanders, Himmler said in October 1943, "The genocide was a proud page in our history.... The death of millions was to preserve our people and our blood....Everything else we can be indifferent to." (Kaden and Nestler *Documente des Verbrechens* vol.1, pp 245-247). Himmler addressed a squad of *Einsatzgruppen*, killing teams of motorized SS troops and said, "You must know what it means to see thousands of corpses laying side-by-side. To have stuck this out is to have kept our integrity. This is what made us hard. In our history, this is an unwritten, and never to be written, page of glory." In other words, don't show off your vile camp.

Wafffen-SS was basically a fighting unit and not just exclusively involved in committing criminal atrocities as the general SS was. The routine reports to the headquarters, the *Waffen* SS, looked mostly like this. "In the conquest of a certain area, the enemy had 100 casualties; no losses among our forces, forty prisoners were taken. The booty was

200 rifles, fifty machine guns 50,000 rounds of rifle ammunition, fifty hand grenades, and 2,000 Jews were shot." Murdering of innocent Jews was a part of the accomplished mission.

Theodor Eicke was pulled out from a psychiatric hospital, and in 1933, Himmler appointed him to be the commander of the first concentration camp, *Dachau*. In his instructions, Himmler implied that "tolerance" meant weakness. Himmler was so pleased with Eicke's performance that in 1934 he appointed Eicke to be Inspector of other Concentration Camps.

The SS worked continuously to cheapen Jewish life by reducing the costs of killing Jews. In some instances, mad dogs were driven to tear the flesh off the victims. In Treblinka, there was a chamber with moving knives where bodies were cut into pieces and then burned. In some instances, Jews had been chased into pounds full of acid. Children were thrown from a cliff into a pit with straw burning on the bottom.

The Holocaust museums in Jerusalem, in Washington, and other places are permanent outcries and reminders against evil. These are shrines for names that were replaced by serial numbers.

The Soviet Union suffered 27 million military and civilian casualties, including the Nazi slaughter of a million Jewish citizens, during WWII. The Holocaust Legacy was not taught in schools. No memorial was commemorated for its 1,300,000 Jewish victimized citizens. The Russian poet, Evgeni Yevtushenko, wrote in his poem about a pit in the Ukraine, at the outskirts of Kiev, of tens of thousand of victims, mostly Jewish, "There is no monument at Babi-Yar, I am frightened...." (A monument has been erected after the collapse of the Soviet Union.)

The savagery during the Holocaust is unparalleled in our world's history. Hitler's political machine used all technological equipment for a systematic extermination of all the people of Jewish heredity. The crimes committed during the Holocaust were of such grave nature that even the maximum sentence or even life sentence for the perpetrators could not do justice to the victims. What would be, for instance, the appropriate punishment for the commandant of Mathausen who murdered 300 people on 4/20/42 as a birthday gift to Hitler? It was quite common practice for the SS to celebrate the Fuhrer's birthday with a sacrifice of Jews. What kind of punishment would suffice for smearing Jewish children's lips with poison?

Furthermore, only a few Nazis were ever held accountable for their crimes against humanity. Many Nazis escaped after the war to Latin American and the Middle-East countries where they have been enjoying a comfortable life. Large numbers of old Nazis are occupying key positions in governmental agencies and in private enterprises, until this very day.

The Holocaust was not only the greatest murder in history but also the greatest theft. As an inheritor, my claim for the property stolen from my parents was declined because I could not substantiate the claim with documents. How could I, when the Germans destroyed the deeds with the owners and possible witnesses of Chrzanów?

"Murder, extermination, and annihilation" are the right words to use when describing what happened during the *Shoah* (Holocasut). Victims were not lost; they did not perish and they did not simply die from natural causes. When you are hunted down with dogs and rifles and thrown into a sealed train taking you to a death factory, you are being murdered. The Nazis installed a conveyor-belt for the systematic annihilation of the Jewish people.

Also, *Shoah* is the correct Hebrew expression for what happened. Holocaust is a complete burning offering in the service of the Temple.

Q: *Do you think that the Holocaust was the worst crime in history?*

HOLOCAUST CRIME

Six million Jews were annihilated in the Holocaust, and so were millions of other people throughout Europe during World War II. Among the victims were one-and-one-half-million Jewish children who had been sent to death camps where their potential, talents, and skills were extinguished. Mankind gained nothing by the consequences of World War II. It was just an absolute human and cultural loss for humanity.

In 1960, the Mossad, Israeli intelligence agents, kidnapped Eichmann in Buenos Aires, Argentina and took him to Israel for trial. During his trial, Eichmann said, **"I must admit that today I regard the extermination of the Jews as one of the worst crimes in the history of mankind."**

Q: *My friend does not believe that the Holocaust actually happened. What should I tell him?*

HOLOCAUST DENIALS

Despite the incontrovertible proof of the horrific atrocities committed during the Holocaust, there are malevolent demagogues that deny the Holocaust, or diminish its enormity. Diminution eventually becomes denial. Die-hard anti-Semites still subscribe to Hitler's racist theories. They deny or distort historical facts.

People who have read historians' books, Holocaust victim's biographies, or visited the Washington, D.C. Holocaust Museum or any other Holocaust museums around the world, are able to rebuke the deniers and revisionists of the Holocaust! The exhibited pictures, obtained mostly from the Nazis and their collaborators and pictures taken by the American, British, French and Russian liberators are all very compelling. Films such as "Schindler's List" provides authentic documentary that is intrinsically educational.

The conclusion that six million Jews were murdered in the Holocaust comes from the Nazis' own accounts. These figures were also established by the International Military Tribunal at Nuremberg. Four million were murdered in camps and two million were murdered by shooting such as in Babi-Yar—starvation and disease in the ghettos of Eastern Europe.

In June 1945, the number of Jews still alive was compared to the number of Jews on record in the municipalities of European countries, prior to the war. In Poland, for example, out of 3,250,000 only 400,000 survived, and 88 percent were murdered. I am the only survivor of my immediate family—one out of five. Five cousins and I are the only survivors out of 128 which is a 5 percent survival rate. From my maternal side, there were no survivors.

In 1958, in Linz, Austria, a performance of the *Diary of Anne Frank* was being disturbed by a gang of juveniles shouting, "This play is a swindle. Anne Frank never lived…Don't believe a word of it. It is all pure invention." Lothar Stelau, from a secondary school in Lübeck who publicly declared the book to be a forgery, was sued by Anne Frank's father. Three experts in court confirmed the authenticity of the book.

Those people who dare to claim that the Holocaust is a hoax are prejudiced or ignorant. No other event in history has been so well-documented as World War II due mainly to the advanced photography. The deniers of the Holocaust ridicule themselves.

I was pleased to read that the British historian, David Irving, a Holocaust denier who describes himself as a "mild fascist", was sentenced on 2/20/2006, to three years in an Austrian prison. Mr. Irving denied the extent of the Holocaust in his speeches given in Austria in 1989. Austria is one of eleven countries that have laws making Holocaust denial a criminal offense.

The German government has recently opened the Nazi archives in Bad Arolsen, Germany. Fifty million files of victims will be available to Holocaust survivors, historians, and others. The records show how and when the six million Jews and others were exterminated.

Only a weak-minded person, being bereft of reason, can deny that the Holocaust did indeed happen. Lies, either expressed verbally or written, can never disguise facts. The truth must be respected! The deniers and revisionists of the Holocaust are rubbing salt on the Holocaust survivors' old wounds and thus hindering healing.

In December 2005, Hisham Abd al-Rauf, a columnist in the Egyptian daily *Al Masaa*, wrote that Nazi execution chambers were no more than rooms to disinfect clothing. I wonder how Mr. Al Masaa would explain the murder of my family and millions of others. They just disappeared?

Q: *Many of my friends know nothing about the Holocaust. Is it disturbing to you?*

HOLOCAUST—PERPETUATION OF ITS LEGACY

Very much indeed! It has recently been reported that Prince Harry of Britain, at a certain event, dressed up in a Nazi uniform, complete with the swastika armband. This was indicative of how little the prince knew World War II history. He has definitely never heard a Holocaust survivor's story.

Films such as *Shoah, Schindler's List, Saving Private Ryan, The Pianist*, and many other documentaries are quite educational. Presentations made by Holocaust survivors are very effective. However, "They are getting about as extinct as the dodo bird." In the future, the Internet sites, the libraries, and the museums will have to be the informative sources. Some historians believe that the Holocaust should be an independent field of study.

There is so much to learn that it took a team of Polish scholars twenty-one years to compile five volumes of "*Auschwitz 1940-1945*" (published in 2001). It describes how Auschwitz was run and who the prisoners were. Out of 1.1 million murdered, 960,000 were Jews.

The significance of the Holocaust legacy is not only a 20th century defining event in Jewish history but it exists in the modern world's history. The Holocaust entails ramifications in racial theory, state-sponsored genocide, political ideology, technology, religious authority, and in many other areas of human and social behavior. Nazism inverted and distorted all the western doctrines of ethics, theology, morality, and philosophy.

If the Jews in Europe had been killed for what they believed in, it becomes imperative that students learn about Jewish history's creativity and its destruction.

It is an integral part of 20th century history.

Q: *Was the world really indifferent to the killing of the Jews in Europe?*

INDIFFERENCE

Most leaders of the world deliberately refrained from acknowledging the mass murder of millions of innocent people during the Holocaust years. The governments let out a sigh but it should have been the epicenter of their agenda!

The International Committee of the Red Cross in Geneva, Switzerland did not intervene even once with the Third Reich government regarding the Jews in concentration camps. The committee considered it to be an internal German matter.

The unmistakable indifference to the suffering of European Jewry was even demonstrated by Britain and the United States. The majority of the public and the governments did not want to hear about the ongoing slaughter and did not want to see an influx of refugees to their countries. Josef Goebbels, Hitler's propaganda minister, told foreign correspondents, "If there is any country that believes that it does not have enough Jews, I shall gladly turn over all our Jews to it." Tragically, there were no takers! All hearts and gates remained closed! This policy contradicted the legacy of Thomas Jefferson, the third president of the United States of America, who in 1801 asked, "Shall we refuse the unhappy fugitives from distress the same hospitality that the savages of the wilderness extended to our forefathers arriving in the land? Shall oppressed humanity find no asylum on this globe?"

People within the U.S.A. did not deluge the State Department with letters of protest.

Our suffering was out of sight and out of their minds. If demonstrations in major cities would have taken place throughout the world against the Nazis' barbaric ideas, then, the large-scale killing and crimes against humanity of the innocent might have been restrained. How could so many give in to such an inhumane ideology in Germany proper and in its occupied lands? The world's indifference tacitly condoned the Nazis' sadistic treatment of the Jews. It led to an unchallenged genocide. In 1940, the United States was still a neutral country, and a powerful protest might have been effective and put off or even stopped the Nazis' destructive machinery in Germany and in the occupied lands.

Here is one example: The Nazis' unhindered atrocities against the Jews inspired other anti-Semites to join the plunder and torment the Jews. In Rumania, under Marshal Ion Antonescu, the Iron Guards emulated the brutality of the Germans "Brown Shirts." In January 1941, Franklin Mott Gunther, the American Representative to Rumania reported to the U.S. State Department a massacre of hundreds of Jews in Bucharest. Sixty Jewish corpses were found hanging on hooks in a slaughterhouse skinned by the Iron Guards. Ignorant primitive young savages with dull vengeful minds had responded to the German-controlled and German-inspired Rumanian press. "It makes one sick at heart to be accredited to a country where such things can happen!" If the United States would have protested the Rumanian persecution, many lives could have been saved, but the U.S. kept silent.

One U.S. diplomat who was not indifferent was Henry Bingham. He defied his bosses in Washington and granted over 2,500 U.S.visas to Jewish and other refugees, including the artists Marc Chagall and Max Ernst, and the family of the writer, Thomas Mann. In 1941, he also sheltered Jews in his Marseilles home, and obtained forged identity papers to help Jews in their dangerous journeys across Europe. He worked with the French underground to smuggle Jews out of France into Franco's Spain or across the Mediterranean, and even contributed to their expenses out of his own pocket.

The United States participated in the 1936 Olympics that took place in Berlin, helping Hitler to feel triumphant. It inadvertently enhanced Hitler's prestige. Had the U.S. refused to participate as a protest against the persecution of the Jewish people and others in Germany, it could have restrained the Nazi racial policies introduced at that time in Germany's Third Reich! Worldwide battle with Hitler's racist and fascist ideas in 1936 could perhaps have prevented battles on the front lines in 1942-1945.

Antithetically, the Danes had proved that widespread resistance to Nazi policies was possible and thus saved Jewish lives. Many individuals from different countries proved that lives could be saved if they were not indifferent. Historically, the U.S. governments and the public did manifest concern and did protest the persecution of Jews, and others overseas, and the intercession helped!

Here are some examples:

Jews were arbitrarily charged with ritual murder of Damascus children in Syria, and many were arrested, tortured, and murdered. The U.S. President, Martin Van Buren, told Secretary of State, John Forsyth, to file a protest with the Sultan of the Ottoman Empire. Consequently, the Sultan issued an order to the judges of Constantinople to release all Jews charged of that murder.

In Russia, 1903—The death of a young Russian boy in Kishinev, Tsarist Russia, was falsely attributed to a Jewish ritual murder, and in an ensuing pogrom many Jews were murdered. Thousand of U.S. citizens of all religions signed and sent to the Czar of Kishinev a Massacre petition. In protest, the House of Representatives voted overwhelmingly to terminate the Treaty of 1832. That protest stopped the killings.

While freedom and human dignity were consumed in the flames of the Holocaust, no fire engines came to extinguish the inferno. A combination of isolationism, diplomatic evasion, raw bigotry, and indifference helped Hitler to carry out genocide against the Jews and many other innocent and defenseless people.

American and European leaders attended a ceremony on 7/11/2005 to commemorate the tenth anniversary of the execution of 7,000 Muslim men and boys by Bosnian Serbs, in Srebrenica. The leaders apologized for not having protected those Muslim victims. I just wondered why the leaders of those same countries never apologized for not protecting or saving the lives of so many millions of innocent victims during the Holocaust. A phenomena well-illustrated is in David Wyman's book, *Abandonment of the Jews*. Another well-written book on this subject is Arthur D. Morse's book, *While 6 Million Died*.

Haile Selassie (1930-1974) was the emperor of Ethiopia. In his address to the General Assembly of the United Nations after World War II, he said, "Throughout history, it has been the inaction of those who could have acted, the indifference of those who should have known better, that the silence of the voice of justice when it mattered most, has made it possible for evil to triumph."

Historical events show clearly that evil can be rooted out only through struggle. It is never through surrender to the aggressor or appeasement of the oppressor. Evil should not be fought with evil, but must be confronted and removed from power. The human brain that distinguishes us from other animals, has a memory capacity that cannot and should not forget its history.

Aristotle (384-322 B.C.) said, "What it lies in our power to do lies in our power not to do." We can be passive, but we also have the ability and moral obligation not to be indifferent to other people's suffering.

The atrocities in ghettos, in forced labor camps, in the killing centers, in concentration camps and in so many places were so horrific that they shattered our faith in human beings, and in the wall of civilization that was supposed to constrain the worst in human behavior. The atrocities and the crimes of Nazi Germany had been vicious, constant, systematic, remorseless, and ubiquitous in Europe, and well-known all over the world. However, the world talked very little about it and the media wrote very little about it.

Niemoller—Pastor Martin Niemoller, who was once an enthusiastic Nazi but later turned into a defender of the Jews once said, "First they came for the communists, and I didn't speak up because I wasn't a communist. Then they came for the Jews, and I didn't speak up because I wasn't a Jew. Then they came for the trade unionists, and I didn't speak up because I wasn't a trade unionist. Then they came for the Catholics and I didn't speak up because I was a Protestant. Then they came for me, and by that time there was nobody left to speak up for me."

I heard an anecdote about an elderly Bedouin leader who thought that by eating turkey he could restore his virility. So he bought a turkey, kept it by his tent, and stuffed it with food every day. One day someone stole his turkey. The Bedouin elder called his sons together and told them, "Boys, we are in great danger. Someone has stolen my turkey." The sons answered back, "Father, what do you need a turkey for?" He responded, "Never mind, just get my turkey back." But the sons ignored him, and a month later someone stole the old man's camel. "What should we do?" the sons asked. "Find my turkey," said the father. But the sons did nothing, and a few weeks later the man's daughter was raped. The old man said to his sons, "It is all because they could get away with my turkey. If we open the window, even just a crack, the cold air of evil spirit will fill the entire room."

We cannot turn aside or be indifferent to dangers in the world. We cannot shirk our responsibility from taking military action because of the potential loss of life and economic resources. We should never flinch at calculating the greater cost of inaction when tyranny reins and our own security is in peril. A passive response to tyranny will not restrain a tyrant from evil.

During World War II, antiwar and isolationist feelings were strong in the U.S. America stood on the sidelines for two years while the Axis armies destroyed the freedom of European countries in a rampage that culminated in the Holocaust. The victims of the Holocaust had bullets in their bodies from the heartless peoples of the world. In 1942, the British intelligence intercepted the German code, and realized that four million Jews had been annihilated; the U.S. government sat on the news.

If the Western democracies during Hitler's regime in the 1930s had taken pre-emptive action to bring down Hitler's regime, one of the worst horrors in history could have been avoided. If no action is taken when the civilized world is faced with similar situations, we are doomed to repeat history. If preventive steps are not taken, the risk of evil will prevail. At best, it postpones them. At worst, it allows nightmares to grow in whatever fashion their lethal ingenuity allows. We know this because they did it again on 9/11/2001.

The world saw the Holocaust as a Jewish problem and not as a human tragedy for an enlightened civilization. Many are guilty by their insouciance. Hitler and his cohorts were audacious because of the fecklessness and indifference to the rest of the world.

Mohandas Gandhi—India's most famous champion of non-violence believed that if the Jews had committed mass suicide, it would have aroused the world to protest Hitler's genocide of the Jewish people. I have my doubts. However, if the people of the democratic nation of the world would have risen in protest, perhaps the slaughter of so many Jewish and non-Jewish could have been stopped.

Zygielbojm—In June 1942, just several days prior to my deportation to forced labor camps, I read about Szmul Zygielbojm's suicide in London. In a letter he left behind, he wrote, among other outcries, "By the passive observation of the murder of defenseless millions and of the maltreatment of children, women, and old men, the Allied States have become the criminal's accomplices.... As I was unable to do anything during my life, perhaps by my death I shall contribute to breaking down that indifference."

If I had carried out my attempted suicide in February 1945, it would have had no effect. I was just a young Jewish slave, a number without a name. Zygielbojm was a prominent Jew, a Socialist member of the Polish Council in England. His suicide apparently did not have much impact either on the hardened hearts of those who could come to the rescue of those doomed by the Nazis. Stefan Zweig, an Austrian Jew, a poet and novelist, committed suicide 1942 in Brazil. What did it change? There were many others who likewise killed themselves out of desperation, and in protest for the world's lack of concern for the Holocaust victims.

Being in camps, we believed that Hitler did what he did to us, what he was allowed to do to us by an indifferent world. Indifference to others' suffering means denying their existence; this is a sin! Compassionate people have no right to remain silent in the face of genocide against any people. If we let the seeds of racism and prejudice be sown, they will sprout and eventually flourish.

Q: *In camps, you had no access to radio, newspapers, and magazines. Why? Why did Hitler ban so many books?*

INFORMATION

In forced labor camps, we were deprived of any printed material, radio, or visual information from any source. In the process of dehumanizing us, the Nazis starved our minds as they starved our bodies.

Hitler and Gobbles ordered the burning of thousands of books. Those bonfires were predicated on the idea that elucidation of other "inferior peoples" could undermine his fascistic armies. Every book where the author's views did not coincide with the Nazis ideology was banned. Among the forbidden authors were Hemingway, Faulkner, and Wolfe, etc. Soviet repression of literature followed the same principle.

The German people were deprived of a reminder of the contributions that victims of the Holocaust could have made, had their lives not been lost to hatred. Perhaps amongst those lost was another Albert Einstein, Isaac Stern, and J. E. Salk, etc.

Q: *You suffered so much. Why is it that you have lived so long? What are your vices?*

LONGEVITY

Well, I do not smoke, I do not drink alcoholic beverages, I am a vegetarian, and I do not take drugs to get high. All this might have contributed to my longevity. I don't know for sure; nobody has an absolute explanation for his or her lifespan.

To address your question as to what my vices are, well, I like chocolate and women.

I was invited to that school for a second time the following year; the teacher gave me a box of candies, saying to me, "I remember your two vices, chocolate and women so I am trying to respond to your chocolate appetite. If you come again next year, we shall see." To which my response was, "As I have stated several times in my presentation; there is always hope, although, by plain arithmetic, you could be my granddaughter."

Q: *As I understand now, no money in the world could have saved your father's life, or could have kept you free. My question is; as a free person now, do you strive to have a lot of money?*

MONEY

I have always been aware of the importance of money in order to sustain oneself and one's family. However, I never had any desire to have a big bank account, or to acquire property. My father's inculcated adages were, "The more property you have, the more worries you have. Do not buy what you want; buy what you need. The real property of man is not what he owns but what he knows. Let people value you for your generosity and not for your bank account. If you do have money and you do not use it wisely, especially to benefit others, you have wasted your time in amassing it."

My father was considered to be rich. Money and wealth granted prestigious status in the community where I grew up. The only people in town who had been more respected and influential than the wealthy were scholars and clergy. The most reputable wealthy citizens in the community were those who led a modest life and donated lavishly to the needy and communal religious institutions.

I witnessed many a time that money, per se, guarantees no health, no happiness, and not even an assurance of survival. Such was the fate of my family during the Holocaust. I have also learned that there is no guarantee for a sustained value of assets just as there is no assurance for staying alive and being healthy. Material pleasures do not guarantee peace of mind. Lack of big money has never hindered my amorous adventures. I shall leave this world as I came into it, with nothing or as much as I was left with when I was stripped of everything in the Waldenburg concentration camp. The only currency we saw in the camps was inflicted pain.

Q: *How do you explain your perseverance and survival under those terrible conditions that you had been subjected to?*

PERSEVERANCE AND SURVIVAL

I am still questioning why my life was spared and not my brothers'. My survival is both an exalted privilege and a painful burden. My body and mind were severely damaged by the Nazis, but not the foundation of my constitution. Therefore, I shall not dwell constantly on the negative memories and aspects of my past experience. I shall not let the poisonous weeds grow in my mind and soul. I must accept the past as the past without forgetting or discarding it. I was knocked down by the Nazis, but I am determined not to remain down for the rest of my life.

Narrow prison walls cannot set limits to our imagination. Study finds that just thinking that a certain medicine will relieve pain is enough for the brain to release its own natural painkillers and soothe painful sensation. There is evidence that the brain's own fighting chemicals, called endorphins, play a role, known as the placebo effect. Just thinking about relief can ease the pain.

"It's difficult in times like these—ideals, dreams and cherished hopes rise within us, only to be crushed by grim reality. It's a wonder I have not abandoned all my ideals, since they seem so impractical. Yet, I cling to them because I still believe, in spite of everything, that most people are truly good at heart." Anne Frank.

Maimonides (1135-1204), a physician, philosopher and a Jewish leader, when facing an option to face death or conversion to Islam said, "Shall I be slain or utter the formula of Islam, I shall utter the formula and live."

Victor Frankl, who was subjected to brutal conditions in concentration camps, still knew inner richness and even happiness while thinking of his beloved ones in past and present. In his book, *Men's Search for Meaning*, he writes that he did find life meaningful even while suffering. Being incarcerated for three years in Auschwitz, the Nazis starved him, beat him, and humiliated him, but they could not control his active mind.

He stored his ideas in his memory, working on his Logotherapy theory. Presuming that his beloved parents and his lovely wife were killed by the Nazis did not stop him from loving his loved ones and entertaining his thoughts with pleasant memories of the past. The goal of life is not to escape it, but to make it holy and meaningful.

Post Traumatic Stress Disorder (PTSD). In slaved labor and concentration camps, I was subjected to witness and personally experienced the most horrific mistreatments. To fight PTSD, I diverted my thoughts to pleasant memories, and tried not to dwell on nightmares.

Happiness can be achieved, villains can be defeated, and the means of success can be learned if you have a positive approach. By contrast, a negative approach may make us wonder why we should risk getting out of bed in the morning; never mind why we should excel in our tasks. A positive attitude was a major component of the survival kit to many in concentration camps

Tuesdays with Morrie is a book about a friendly relationship between the student, Mitch Albom, and his favorite professor, Morrie Schwartz of Brandeis University. Morrie was so full of life that he danced by himself if no partner was at hand. Morrie had amyotrophic lateral sclerosis (ALS), Lou Gehrig's—a brutal illness of the neurological system; it is terminal. He continued to teach as long as possible. The idea of quitting did not occur to Morrie. "Do I wither up and disappear, or do I make the best of my time left?"

We should always be reminded that life is good, and that it is challenging and full of exciting possibilities. As vitamins and minerals are essential to our physical health, so is a positive attitude vital to our mental health.

Living with a clean conscience and free of a guilt feeling is the best prescription for a happy life. In spite of all the humiliation, hunger, and beatings, etc., it was possible for spiritual life to thrive. Some inmates were able to retreat from their terrible surroundings to a life of inner richness and spiritual freedom. They found an aesthetic potential in the most unfavorable situation. I tried to revel in memories of my warmly embracing family back home.

Q: *Could you pray when you were in camps? I am Jewish, but I seldom go to the synagogue. When you were a kid, did you go to the synagogue everyday? Am I a sinner if I do not pray?*

PRAYER

At home, in Chrzanów, our daily routine centered on fulfilling religious tenets, rituals and three daily prayers at the synagogue or at home. I remember watching my father and my older brother, bound around their head and left forearm the Tefillin, leather phylacteries (small black leather cubes that contain four biblical phrases from the Torah, the Pentateuch.) This obligatory ritual has to be practiced every weekday morning by every man, starting at the age of thirteen. My father had purchased Tefillin for me, but tragically, he was murdered one month prior to my thirteenth birthday.

I enjoyed all the festivities and abided by all the sacred duties expected of a young boy. I shivered with awe when I watched the fervor of older men praying. It was a profound inspiration but difficult for me to articulate. The synagogue was not just a house of prayer and study but a venue imbued with intellectual and social ferment. Religious observance was an integral part of the Jewish community. The staid services were intertwined with chants by a leader or cantor. Occasionally, choirs took part in the service. I was a choir boy for a short time. The synagogue was my favorite place, not just spiritually, but as the center for meeting peers and making new friends. For my father, the synagogue was also a traditional frontier between rest and toil. For me, it was a school away from school. There were no special services for the young, as it is provided today in some synagogues. Boys attended services in the main sanctuary where their fathers worshipped. Women and girls listened to the services conducted in the men's section of the synagogue. A structured wall separated the sexes. Since there were no microphones, I wondered how well the women could follow the services.

There is always something to be thankful for while praying, even under the most horrible circumstances as illustrated in the following dialogue. During the Holocaust, a religious inmate who had been praying was asked by another inmate who was a non-believer, "What are you praying for?" "I am thanking God" was the answer! "For being in this hell?" challenged the secular inmate." "Yes, I am thanking God for not making me like them, the Nazis!"

When the second temple was destroyed in 70 C.E., and the Israelites were forced to leave the land, prayer replaced the ritual sacrifice that used to be offered in the temple. In camps, we could only pray by heart because the Nazis put our *siddurim* (prayer books) in their bonfire. It reminds me of Rabbi Abraham Herschel from New York, who marched alongside the Rev. Martin Luther King, Jr. during the civil rights movement. He said that he felt his feet were praying; so were my withered feet praying while marching to work in Germany. On Yom Kippur, the Day of Atonement, I was praying and fasting even though I had become prone to die of starvation.

I felt sometimes that "I was the man who had known affliction under the 'rod of God's wrath' as quoted in Lamentations 3:1. Quite often while suffering in concentration camps and unable to understand the infliction, I talked to myself like Job (Job 9.34). I would pray, "If only God would take His rod away from me."

Having no calendars, several pious men kept memorizing the Hebrew calendar. When marching to and from the working place, I was praying and supplicating God to lessen my misery. God did not answer our prayers when we were hungry, cold, and tortured. One roommate, a very pious man, stopped praying. He lost faith in the divine. I was pondering if the less devout will persevere. "*Im bearazim nafla salhevet ma yasu azovei kir*" —If cedars have caught fire, what will the moss on the wall do? If the mighty, the pious ones have succumbed, how shall the weak, the less observant, emerge unscathed?

It was the Nazis intention to humiliate us, and to extinguish any shred of faith that we might have had. They wished to turn us into despicable bodies without a soul. However, the faithful sprinkled the drudgery of daily life with prayer, which invigorated them with hope.

The call for prayer came from within the soul. Prayer was never imposed. It is mentioned in yesterday's paper that an Islamic court in Somalia issued an edict that anybody who is not praying five times a day will be beheaded. I was supplicating God when I felt the need for it.

For three years, in forced labor and concentration camps, I questioned God as to what I had done to deserve so much suffering. I had been pondering what God's intention was. What was His message behind that ordeal? I often cried while praying but the heavens seemed silent. All fateful events that took place during my incarceration were absolutely beyond my control, just as earthquakes or tsunamis are beyond any mortals' control. It seemed to me that there was a special path or a certain prayer for knowing how to reach God. I just did not know it. Thus, God didn't hear me

On the way to work, I cited Birchat-Haboker, the Morning Prayer: "Blessed are you God who clothes the naked; blessed are you God who did not make me a slave." Ironically, I had no warm cloth; I was freezing and I was a slave.

Q: *I know that prejudice is not good. I see it often in my school and in my neighborhood. How can it be eradicated?*

PREJUDICE

The best definition for prejudice would be an unfavorable opinion formed beforehand without knowledge. In other words, you are having a hostile attitude regarding a racial, religious or national group that stems from ignorance. Only a person who lacks certain knowledge or information about the targeted group may be tempted to prejudge those of other ethnicities. A fight against prejudice and ignorance is not just worth waging but it is imperative.

Just as we have a warning system of an approaching hurricane, we should be on alert whenever seeds of racial bigotry are sprouting. Just as vulnerable residents are advised to evacuate the area that might be affected by the hurricane, so should the governments and peoples stop the sowing of hatred by depraved characters! Perhaps incitement for bias should be considered indecent, to be subjected to a fine as broadcasters in the U.S. face a penalty if they do not clean up their programs to assure parents that their children won't be exposed to inappropriate material.

The smallest seedling of violence, nurtured by hate, must be torn out by its roots the moment it is spotted. Prejudice is not a character flaw; it is a contagious disease. It poisons the well of humanity. Objective enlightenment will obviate the folly of prejudice. **Tolerance is the healing balm for our deeply troubled world.**

Stereotyping or sweeping guilt by association is essentially unfair and illogical.

Q: *You mentioned that your friend was hidden by a Polish family and survived the war. Did your friend have to pay for it?*

A RIGHTEOUS FAMILY

Yehudah E., a good friend of mine who lives in Israel, survived the war in hiding. He and two young Jewish men were hidden for over two years by the Wiglush family in Kanczuga, Poland. The Germans executed another Polish family of eight from the same village of Kanczuga for hiding a Jew. Five-hundred-and-twenty-one Polish families were executed for sheltering Jews. Mr. Erlich's saviors were not deterred, despite the grave risk to their own family. When the war ended, the Wiglush family did not ask to be recompensed for jeopardizing the very survival of the entire Wiglush family. The head of the household felt rewarded by managing to save innocent lives.

There were many anti-Semites in Poland. Some even collaborated with the Nazis. This case is just another compelling example that no ethnic group or nation can be painted with the same brush. There are righteous people and some wicked people in every group.

Yad—Vashem, the Holocaust Memorial in Jerusalem, Israel recognized the Wiglush family to be among the righteous in the alley of those who risked their lives to save others' lives. People like Mr. Wiglush did not save lives because they expected recognition. They risked their own lives to save others because it was the right thing to do. For the last sixty years, Mr. Ehrlich has been in contact with the Wiglush family and its descendants. As a token of appreciation, Mr. Ehrlich has been helping them financially to the best of his ability.

Q: *Were teenagers like you sexually active in Poland? How about in concentration camps?*

SEXUAL ACTIVITY

I was brought up in a religious home, and in a very prudish ambiance. There was a night table between my parent's two beds, as it was in all religious homes. The public and parochial schools that I attended were not co-educational. As a young boy, I interacted mostly with other boys. I seldom exchanged words with little girls. Sex was neither taught in school, nor at home. It was not a topic for discussion. In today's common parlance, the prom is a time to lose one's virginity.

An event that is supposed to be a dance has the flavor of a honeymoon. In my times, there were no proms and no premarital sexual activity. To the best of my recollection, daily papers did not dwell much on sexual activities and there were no sex books, or salacious magazines, or any other prurient material in my family's bookcases.

In retrospect, I wonder why sex education was taboo since the Bible dealt quite explicitly with intricacies of sexuality. I did not experience the pleasures and problems that sexually-active teenagers experience today. Being curious, I used to look through the keyhole of my parent's bedroom to spy on them during their customary Sabbath siesta.

I do remember episodes pertaining to sexual sensations and scandals happening in my little town of Chrzanów.

While strolling one evening in an open field, I inadvertently stepped on a couple making love. I sensed that I had spoiled their "sinful" but delightful time and I ran for my life to escape the man's rage. At home in my solitude, I toyed with images of that encounter. Living in a covered-up culture, this was the first time I saw a woman's breast.

At the age of twelve, I overheard the following story:

Mr. Kaufman, who owned and operated a grocery, told his wife that he was not feeling well. She urged him to go home (located above the store) and lie down. Several hours later, she became concerned because Mr. Kaufman did not return to the store, so she went up to check on him. To her shock, she found her husband in bed with their housemaid. Since there were no means of communication, such as a telephone, in order to call a policeman or a doctor, she opened the window and screamed, "People of mercy, come to my rescue!" Apparently, the lovers could not be separated and Mrs. Kaufman was devastated. The entire town gossiped about the incident for weeks and my father derived a special pleasure from that sensational scandal because Mr. Kaufamn was my father's business competitor. It had spoiled Mr. Kaufamn's reputation of being a pious man and a faithful husband.

In slave labor camps, living conditions left no room for sexual activity or even salacious thoughts. My body was deprived of basic nutrients and the mind was occupied with worries about survival of loved ones and self-preservation. In the environment where there was absolutely no privacy, I did not notice any inmates engaging in recreational sex. In captivity, I was never the object of a sexual advance. Since there were no females in any of the camps where I had been incarcerated, no procreative sex could have taken place. Needless to say, I was not a Romeo and there was no Juliet around. I do not recall fantasizing about romance or sexual prurience. Starvation and humiliation permeated my existence.

I was not aware of any sexual abuses such as individual or gang rape. When starvation was prevalent, sex offense among the inmates could not flourish despite the diversity of age and perhaps different sexual orientation. I presume that we were all prone to an erectile dysfunction.

Q: *It might be a silly question, but I shall ask anyway. You have suffered so much. How is it that you have that constant smile?*

SMILING

It is one component of my survival kit. However, I do not have a constant smile at all times. I am very careful in whose presence I smile. Let me tell you why.

A pastor visited one of his congregants in the hospital and said, "Keep smiling, Joe, we are praying for you and you will be okay."

Joe retorted, "I am not going to listen to you this time, reverent."

"Why?" asked the clergyman."

"You see, reverend, I was smiling at my neighbor's wife, so her husband beat me up, and that is the reason for me being in the hospital."

A high school student asked me once, "How come somebody who had suffered so much as you did is able to smile?"

My response was, "My smiling face does not indicate that my heart stopped bleeding. In fact, it has indeed been bleeding for the last sixty-seven years. I am just sending a message to Hitler and to those who had been following his racist ideology that the Nazis' plan to stop me breathing at the age of thirteen did not materialize. At the age of eighty, I am breathing and smiling."

Q: *You said that you attended public school in the morning and religious school in the evening, six days a week. Did you have time for sport games?*

SPORTS

I have not participated in any sport games. Sports were not part of the curriculum, either in the elementary public school that I attended or in the religious school. Occasionally, soccer was played by amateurs, and took place in open fields (no stadiums). In those times, it would not have been appropriate for a schoolboy to watch. It would have been deemed a waste of time. Remember, I come from a different culture than the one you know.

In the U.S., I have not learned the rules of any popular sport games. I do not watch sport games on television because it never spurred my interest. I failed to take my sons to see a game or to encourage them to learn how to play any sports games. They rightfully complained about it. I am sorry for neglecting that part of the American culture.

Q: *When you see on TV, or read in the newspaper that people are dying from starvation in Africa and other places on the globe; how do you feel about it?*

STARVATION

I was undernourished during the first two years of World War II, and starving while being incarcerated for three years in concentration camps. I had witnessed thousands of people dying of starvation—a terrible way to die. Watching the dying, I was pondering, "When will it happen to me?!"

Obviously, I am sensitive to other peoples' suffering from hunger, and I am upset and saddened when I hear or read that people nowadays are dying of starvation due to famine, strife, or political conflict around the world.

The Hebrew word for war is *milchama*, the root is *lechem*, which means bread. In other words, wars were being fought for the availability of bread, for provisions to sustain life. When an innocent person is being killed or injured, I ache. When I see on TV images of human suffering, it reminisces the suffering that I had witnessed and experienced.

I yearn for a peaceful day and for a peaceful world. Albert Schweitzer, the French philosopher and physician said, "The soldiers' graves are the greatest preachers of peace." Having been

raised from the ashes of the Holocaust, I pray everyday for peace among nations, peace among men, and the eradication of hunger.

Q: *Hitler was a terrible tyrant, and history is full of them. Do you find any similarity between the tyrants of today and Hitler? Is there such a thing as a benevolent tyrant?*

TYRANNY

Hitler, Stalin, Mao, and Pol Pot were responsible, in the 20th century, for the death of millions upon millions of people. Tragically, there are rulers in the 21st century who would not hesitate to commit genocide. Tyrants are megalomaniacs, malignant narcissists. Self-aggrandizement and hedonistic pleasure propel their behavior. Megalomaniacs thrive when motivated by hatred, including one's own family members, and care little about their own people, as long as it serves their narcissistic trait. War appeals to the vanity of tyrants and their thirst for glory. They do not care for human values and human aspirations in their own nation and other lands. Their lethal regimes will use any ruse, dodges, tricks, cunning, veiling of truth, concealments, assassinations, and genocide, etc. to achieve their ends. In brief, these dangerous leaders of extreme self-absorption and paranoia have no constraints of conscience and will use any means necessary to achieve their goals. Tyrannical regimes do not allow a horizontal conversation—just a vertical, top-down monologue.

Authoritarian governments deprive their people of a voice and the ability to achieve their full potential. An old method and an effective one of tyrannical regimes was first to eliminate internal rivals and then create or invent outside enemies. A ruthless dictatorship intrinsically outlaws decency and brings ostensible stability and efficiency. An amoral and calculating tyrant is sometimes capable of unifying a nation. Tragically, some people do not value freedom and accept dictatorship. To justify repression and retain stability amidst its citizenry, totalitarian regimes perpetuate conflict with external elements to avoid dissent from within, and to shape the minds of their citizens. If there is no enemy, tyrants will create one in order to spur a patriotic fervor among their people.

TYRANNY THRIVES ON HOSTILITY

Hitler used untrammeled terror in order to squash any opposition or dissent. He was not driven by sincere idealism but by hunger for power. His ego was at the core of his political agenda. Hitler and his cohorts, such as the Gestapo and the SS, spawned fear among its citizens turning them into informers: Gentiles against Jews and foreigners, students against teachers, children against parents, and neighbor against neighbor, etc.

Totalitarian regimes destroy the normal patterns of social cohesion. Tyrants rule by subjugating the public, and consequently, people become brutish. Tyranny breeds hatred. Criminal elements flourish and the regime exploits social misery. If a citizen is not allowed to read or say unfavorable things about the ruler of the land he lives in, then that person does not live in a civil society. Under such circumstances, the citizen becomes a prisoner of tyranny, intolerance, and ignorance. The efflorescence of cultural creativity is being suffocated. The tyrant's lust to dominate stifles the spirit of the subjugated citizenry. The ideology of most tyrants has failed. Regretfully, some linger on. Some neo-Nazis cling to the relics of fascism but hopefully it will die with their propagators. **Tyranny is the fruit of hate. Tyrants typically make no demands of themselves. They just demand from others and impose upon others.**

Q: Every day you remember the loved ones you had lost in the Holocaust. So, do you still observe Yom-Hashoa?

YOM HASHOA

Yom Hashoa is Holocaust Remembrance Day that we mark every year on the twenty-seventh day of Nissan (Jewish calendar). On April 16, 2007, we shall again commemorate the tragedy of the Jews of Europe during the Second World War. Let me read to you my address to congregants at Neveh Shalom Synagogue in Portland Oregon, on 4/28/2003.

All of us were overwhelmed with shock and grief by the terrible events of September 11. For me, the date of that tragedy was reminiscent of our family's tragedy when my father was murdered on 9/11, in the year 1939 by German soldiers, who had thrown my father's body into a pit with thirty-six other victims. Three months later, as a thirteen-year-old boy, I was present when my father's partially decomposed body was exhumed—a gruesome and traumatic sight that has been etched in my memory ever since. The horrific scenes on 9/11/2001 evoked disastrous images I had to face sixty-two years earlier. Watching the collapse of the two WTC towers, I wondered, "Will all those people consumed in that inferno have a grave?" Apparently not, just as hundreds of relatives of my extended family, six million Jews, and many World War II victims of other nationalities have no graves to lay wreaths on and no anniversary of the demise of their loved ones.

It is ironic that Hitler did not have a funeral and does not have a grave. Muhammed Attah, one of the nineteen participants in the 9/11/2001 catastrophe left a testament, saying, "At my funeral, I do not want impure beings, especially pregnant women." He had no funeral.

The Nazis seized the photos of my family members and of me. They discarded my birth certificate and gave me no death certificates of my family members that they had murdered. On Holocaust Remembrance Day, we commemorate those innocent men, women and children who were murdered in Auschwitz, Belzec, Chelmno, Maidanek, Sobibor and Treblinka. We mourn those who were slaughtered by the Nazis in slave labor camps, in the ravines of Babi-Yar in the Soviet Union and many Jewish communities in other countries of Europe. We honor the memory of those who fought and died in the Warsaw Ghetto Uprising, in partisan units, and other enclaves of Jewish heroic resistance to the Nazis and their collaborators.

We are here to remember the Avremalechs, Ruchalechs, Moishelechs, Suralechs, one-and-a-half million young Jewish children, and babies ripped from their mothers' arms into the Zyklon B gas chambers, under the guise of shower installations, without a flutter of remorse.

The Holocaust and episodes of mass murder should not be seen as an aberration that will not recur. Vast scales of killing in the twentieth century was more common than in any other era in history. More human beings died in ethnic conflicts, civil strife, and world wars than in all other centuries combined. We have to remember that under Hitler's rein, every Jew was a victim but not every victim was a Jew.

Nowadays we live in an era of automation, digitization, and computerization of almost everything. We are able to reach the moon but unable to reach peace on earth. Many destructive and evil forces prevail in many places of the globe.

For the last two years, I have been sharing my life story with students in high schools and colleges, and with adults in churches and prisons. The most frequent request from my audiences is, "Please continue to share your experience as long as you are able to."

Warner Pacific College awarded me an Honorary Bachelor degree because the faculty and the students felt that the survivors' messages were so educationally relevant. A ninth grader in Sandy, Oregon, who contemplated suicide because of problems she had to face at home, changed her mind after my presentation. She realized that despite all her difficulties, she was still blessed by having everything that I as a teenager had been deprived of. A tenth grader in Hillsboro decided not to drop out of high school after realizing that she was indeed privileged to get an education after hearing that I could not go to school at her age, even though I wanted to. An inmate, a Vietnam War Veteran in a Salem penitentiary told me, "If I would have heard your story thirty years ago, I would have appreciated what I had and not have done something foolish that put me in this hole". A visually-impaired student wrote me, "I just realize how lucky I am to have been born in the U.S. Had I been born in Germany, the Nazis would have murdered me at infancy."

On their way to the crematoriums, some of the victims uttered those last words, "*Shma Israel*—Hear O God of Israel." Other victims were crying and pleading with the apathetic leadership of the religious and secular world, in a medley of tongues.

"Rescue us, remember us, *Gedenkt unz, Zychru otanu, pamietaj nas, Ne felejes el bennunket* remember us, remember the Nazi's cruelty, the *Amalek* of that day (The Amalekites, aboriginal people of Canaan, waged war against the Hebrews Ex 27.8-16, Sam 30.3-20)."

We Holocaust survivors do remember. Our physical and mental scars are constant reminders. However, as the Holocaust moves from living memory into the archives, and as the ranks of Holocaust survivors are rapidly dwindling, 100 of us survivors, and 1,300 World War II veterans die every day in the U.S. —a drastic change is taking place in the landscape of remembrance. It becomes imperative that our children, the second generation, who live in the shadow of the Holocaust, and future generations of all peoples assume the holy task of reminding and remembering the legacy of the Holocaust while simultaneously striving incessantly to divert the rivers of hatred so that another **Holocaust should never, never, never happen again!**

EPILOGUE

If the cataclysmic invasion of German forces into Poland would not have taken place (on 9/1/1939), and the Jews who lived in Chrzanów had never been destroyed, I would have no grounds to write my autobiography at the age of eighty. My life would have probably been uneventful.

I would have definitely graduated from elementary, high school, and even higher.

I would have been religiously observant and erudite in Talmudic studies.

I would have been married by a matchmaker, to a woman whom my parents approved.

I would have probably been involved, and later on inherited my father's business.

I would have probably had my beloved and immediate family until my mid-life years.

I would have been surrounded by my relatives, most of whom lived in Chrzanów.

A SENSELESS DEPRIVATION DUE TO MY FAITH AND FATE

Whoever mulls over my deprivations should appreciate her or his situation.

When I was thirteen years old, the Germans invaded Poland and:

- They shot my father and let him bleed until he expired.

- They forbade me to go to the school that I loved.

- They forbade me to walk in certain streets
  that I knew since I was a little kid.

- I had to wear an armband with a Jewish star
  to be a conspicuous target to be hit.

- I could no longer pray in a house of worship,
  and I could no longer nurture friendship.

- The Germans locked the synagogues and they felt no shame.

- I was ordered to remove my cap and bow
  to every German passing by.

- I had pangs of hunger for many days and
  nights, and I lost all my human rights.

When I was fourteen years old:

- The Germans deported my older brother to a Slave Labor Camp.

When I was fifteen years old:

- The Germans deported me to a Slave Labor Camp.

From the age of fifteen to the age of eighteen :

- Blechhammer, Brande, Gross-Maslowitz, Kletetndorf and
  Waldenburg were the five camps which had been the bane
  of my life, where I spent three years—my school years.

- There was no one to touch me affectionately
  or to be touched by me.

- I was subjected to starvation, sickness,
  sadistic terror and systematic murder.

- My belly was swollen and sore from hunger.

- In Waldenburg, the Nazis took away my
  name and gave me a number.

- I was isolated there; and I saw no woman,
  no child, and not even a flower.

- I had not seen a fresh vegetable or fruit for three years.

- I subsisted on a starvation diet for all those war years.

- I received no medical help; and some doctors
  had no scruples to become executioners.

- They disavowed their Hippocratic Oath
  even when I pleaded with tears.

- The bunk I slept on served as a chair to
  sit on and a table to eat on.

- There were no dishes, no cups, and no glasses;
  just one metal bowl for all purposes.

- There was not a mattress, nor pillows, no
  bed sheets on the bunk I slept on.

- Straw that was infested with cockroaches and
  lice—that was the bed I slept on.

- There was not a pencil or pen to write
  with, nor a paper to write on.

- I had no books; I had no newspapers; I did not
  know what in the world was going on.

- The Nazis starved my body and kept my mind in a blind alley.

- I was never free from ominous fear.

- There was no privacy in the latrine and
  there was no toilet paper.

- Everything I had to do had to be done in a rush.

- I had no towel, no comb, and no toothbrush.

- I could not see my face because there was no
  mirror; all my eyes saw was horror.

- I did not live; I could hardly exist; the
  only right I had was to die.

- I had no watch to know the time, no calendar to
  know the date, and no holidays to celebrate.

- I could not send or receive letters; I could
  not use a phone to communicate,

- I worked very hard and long hours, almost
  every day but never, never for pay.

- I had no warm clothes, no socks, no
  boots—just a wooden-soled shoe.

- In winter, I shivered in the cold and turned blue.

- At work, I was forbidden to eat, drink, or talk.

- When nature called, I had to ask permission to take a walk.

- Beasts were better off than me, believe you me.

- I was agonized by the sense of loneliness and helplessness.

- We became the subjects of a psychopathic
  tyrant; slaves of exploiters and monsters.

- Hitler deemed non-Aryans to be chaff, to be
  subjugated, and eventually annihilated.

- By what criteria was I inferior, by not
  having blue eyes and blond hair?

- I wondered why nobody came to my rescue.

When I was liberated by the Russian Army, at the age of eighteen:

- I weighed eighty pounds—just skin and bones—a skeleton.

- I had no family, no money, no skills, and no home.

- I was the only survivor of my immediate family—so sad to be alone.

- I was told that my stepmother and her nine-year-old son, my brother, were deported to Auschwitz on 2/18/43. They perished there soon after their arrival; so did my grandparents, uncles, aunts and cousins.

None of my hundreds of close and distant relatives had a funeral. There were no graves and no anniversaries of their demise. I have ceased to see their faces and hear their voices. This bitter reality burns through the fabric of my life like a scorching beam. I am the only one left to cry for all of them. Still, I am determined not to be bitter but better. The Germans enslaved me for three years, but I am determined not be enslaved to anger for the rest of my life. In my adolescent years, I could not learn to read and write, learn how to swim, fish, play ball, and discover the world. I could not discover myself, discover girls, and become a man. I am still trying to catch up with the losses of those precious years and it has not been easy.

Just as the homosexuals, the Jehovah's Witnesses, communists and others were murdered not for what they had done or said, but for what they were. I was a victim of insane cruelty for no offense or sin—just for my faith. I was condemned though never accused of any offense.

I have been clamoring to know why! Sometimes I wish I could pretend that it did not happen, but it did. Regretfully, it may happen again if we let prejudice and evil rein.

Count your blessings!

CPSIA information can be obtained
at www.ICGtesting.com
Printed in the USA
FSHW011300131218
54446FS